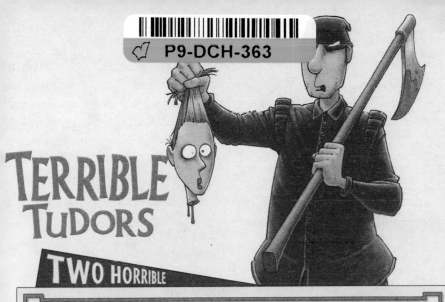

TERRIBLE TUDORS

TWO HORRIBLE

HORRIBLE HISTORIES

BOOKS IN ONE

SLIMY STUARTS

TERRY DEARY & NEIL TONGE
ILLUSTRATED BY MARTIN BROWN

SCHOLASTIC

Scholastic Children's Books,
Euston House, 24 Eversholt Street,
London, NW1 1DB, UK

A division of Scholastic Ltd
London ~ New York ~ Toronto ~ Sydney ~ Auckland
Mexico City ~ New Delhi ~ Hong Kong

First published in the UK in this edition by Scholastic Ltd, 1997
This edition published 2009

Some of the material in this book has previously been published in
Horrible Histories The Massive Millennium Quiz Book/Horribly Huge Quiz Book

Text copyright © Terry Deary, 1996, 1999
Illustrations © Martin Brown, 1996, 1999
All rights reserved

ISBN 978 1407 10971 8

Page layout services provided by Quadrum Solutions Ltd, Mumbai, India
Printed in the UK by CPI Bookmarque, Croydon, CR0 4TD

4 6 8 10 9 7 5 3

The right of Terry Deary and Martin Brown to be identified as the author and illustrators of this work respectively has
been asserted by them in accordance with the Copyright, Designs and Patents Act, 1988.

CONTENTS

Terrible Tudors

CONTENTS

Slimy Stuarts

TERRIBLE TUDORS

Introduction

If you think history is horrible then this is the book for you!

Sometimes history lessons in school can be horribly boring…

Sometimes it can be horribly confusing…

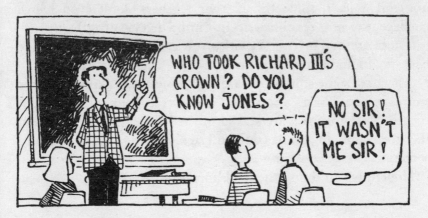

And sometimes history can be **horribly** unfair…

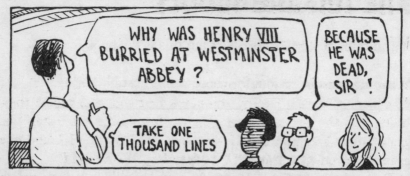

But this book is about **really horrible** history. It's full of the sort of facts that teachers never bother to tell you. Not just the bits about the kings and the queens and the battles and the endless lists of dates – it's also about the ordinary people who lived in Tudor times. People like you and me. Commoners! (Well, I'm dead common, I don't know about you!)

And what made them laugh and cry, what made them suffer and die. **That's what this book will try to help you understand**. You might learn some things your teachers don't even know! (Believe it or not, **teachers do not know everything!**)

There are one or two activities you can try. That's about the best way to find out what it was like to be a common Tudor.

There are some stories that are as chilling as the chilliest horror stories in your library. (You may have to read them with the light turned off in case you are scared of the shadows!) The facts and the stories should amaze you and teach you and amuse you, and sometimes make you sad.

Hopefully you'll find them all **horribly interesting**.

The terrible Tudors

What is a terrible Tudor?

What your teacher will tell you...
The Tudors were a family who ruled England, and poked their noses into the rest of Great Britain, from 1485 till 1603. The grandfather was Henry VII, his son was Henry VIII and the grandchildren were Edward VI, Mary I and Elizabeth I.

Five rulers and 118 years that changed the lives of the English people.

Who's who?

Henry VII (Henry Tudor of Lancaster) King from 1485 to 1509 Defeated King Richard III at the Battle of Bosworth and took his crown. Married Elizabeth of York to stop their two families ~~whingeing~~ scrapping over the crown.

HENRY VII

Henry VIII King from 1509 to 1547
Son of Henry VII. Wanted a son to keep the Tudor line going and he didn't care how many wives he had till he got one.

HENRY VIII

When he got rid of his first wife by divorcing her, the head of the Catholic Church (the Pope I didn't approve of it... so Henry made his own church (the Church of England), with himself as the head.

Henry got rid of the Catholic monasteries with their monks and nuns. (The money he got for their riches came in very handy!) But he still worshipped as a Catholic, and chopped off the heads of those who didn't.

~ HENRY VIII's WIVES ~

GOOD WIFE GUIDE

CHILDREN		WHAT HAPPENED	
👧 GIRL 👦 BOY		🗡️ DIVORCED	✝️ DIED
😟 NO CHILDREN		🪓 BEHEADED	👑 SURVIVED

CATHERINE OF ARAGON
QUEEN · Apr 1506 to Apr 1533 — Mary I — *divorced*

ANNE BOLEYN
QUEEN · Jan 1533 to May 1536 — Elizabeth I — *beheaded*

JANE SEYMOUR
QUEEN · May 1536 to Oct 1537 — Edward VI — *died*

ANNE OF CLEVES
QUEEN · Jan 1540 to July 1540 — no children — *divorced*

CATHERINE HOWARD
QUEEN · July 1540 to Feb 1541 — no children — *beheaded*

CATHERINE PARR
QUEEN · July 1543 to Jan 1547 — no children — *survived*

Anne Boleyn's last words before she had her head chopped off were **not**, "I'll just go for a walk around the block!"

Edward became king first, even though he was the youngest. That's because a male child always took the throne before a female child. The same rule still applies in England.

EDWARD VI

Edward VI King of England from 1547 to 1553
Was too young to rule, so had a Protector, the Duke of Somerset, to "help" him out. King Edward was engaged to Mary Queen of Scots, but this fell through. Just as well, really, as Edward was a Protestant and Mary a Catholic, which would have caused big problems. The Duke of Northumberland, made Edward get rid of Somerset. Northumberland became the next Protector - what a surprise! Poor Edward was a sickly lad and died of tuberculosis at the age of 16.

Lady Jane Grey Queen of England in 1553
Put on the throne by Northumberland, who had persuaded Edward to make her his heir because she was a Protestant, and was great grand-daughter of Henry VII. She was also Northumberland's daughter-in-law! Lady Jane sat on the throne for nine days then Mary Tudor raised an army and walloped Northumberland. So Lady Jane was pushed off her throne and her head was pushed on the block.

LADY JANE GREY

Mary I (Mary Tudor) Queen of England 1553 to 1558

Was a devout Catholic, so she made the Pope head of the English church again. Married King Philip of Spain, also a Catholic. People were frightened of Philip's power, and the marriage led to Wyatt's rebellion, which was crushed by Mary's army. Philip, never short of an idea or two, persuaded Mary to fight the French. The English lost. Mary was getting more unpopular by

MARY I
(MARY TUDOR)

the minute, but was probably too insane to care. Ended up with the nickname 'Bloody Mary', owing to regular head-choppings and burnings of Protestants.

ELIZABETH I

Elizabeth I Queen of England from 1558 to 1603

Had pretended to be a Catholic while Mary Tudor was Queen, just to keep her happy. But changed both herself and England into Protestants when she came to the throne. Locked up Mary Queen of Scots and chopped off her head because she was a Catholic, and because Catholic Europe thought that Mary should be Queen of England. Elizabeth never married, because she said that she was married to England! But she had a definite soft spot for the Earl of Essex, which didn't stop her from having **his** head chopped off as well.

Terrible Tudor Limericks

Confused? You may be, but try learning these limericks, and you'll easily remember...

Henry VII

Henry Tudor beat Richard the Thirder
When the battle turned into pure murder.
Henry pinched Richard's crown
For the ride back to town.
He was top man! He could go no furder.

Henry VIII

King Henry was fat as a boar
He had six wives and still wanted more.
Anne and Kate said,
"By heck! He's a pain in the neck!"
As their heads landed smack on the floor.

Edward VI

At nine years the little King Eddie
Had a grip on the throne quite unsteady.
He was all skin and bone,
Grown men fought for his throne
And by sixteen young Eddie was deadie.

Mary I

Bloody Mary, they say, was quite mad.
And the nastiest taste that she had
Was for protestant burning
Seems she had a yearning
To kill even more than her dad.

Elizabeth I

A truly great queen was old Lizzie,
She went charging around being busy.
She thought herself beaut,
But her teeth looked like soot
And her hair it was all red and frizzy.

Terrible Tudor times

1485 – reign of Henry VII

Henry Tudor beat King Richard III at the Battle of Bosworth Field and became the first Tudor king. The Wars of the Roses ended – they had been dividing the country for over 30 years.

1487 A boy called Lambert Simnel claims to be king. His revolt fails. Is given a job in the palace kitchens!

1492 Christopher Columbus lands in America – the world is never the same again!

1497 Perkin Warbeck tries to take the English throne. Warbeck hanged in 1499. England settles down under Henry VII and becomes richer and more peaceful than in the past.

1509 – reign of Henry VIII

1516 Mary I born – daughter of Henry VIII's Catholic first wife, Catherine of Aragon.

1517 First real Protestant revolt against the Catholic Church begins in Germany.

1520 Henry VIII appears at the Field of the Cloth of Gold – a ceremonious meeting between Henry and Francis I of France.

1533 Elizabeth I born, daughter of Henry's second wife, Anne Boleyn.

1534 Henry takes over as head of the Church in England.

1535 Henry begins to execute Catholics who object to his Church takeover.

1536 Anne Boleyn, (Elizabeth I's mother) executed and Henry begins to close down monasteries. 1537 Edward VI born – but his mother dies shortly afterwards. Edward is always a weak child.

1547 – reign of Edward VI

1547 Edward VI just nine years old when he takes the throne.

The Duke of Somerset runs the country for the boy. His title is 'Protector'.

1549 Kett's rebellion in Norfolk against the new Protestant king.

1550 The Duke of Somerset executed and replaced by Duke of Northumberland as the new Protector.

1553 Edward is ill. He is persuaded to name Lady Jane Grey as the next Queen - this is partly to stop the Catholic Mary getting her hands on the throne... but the plan doesn't work. Young Ed dies.

1553 – reign of Mary I

Mary tries to return England to the Catholic faith. She has over 300 Protestants burned.
1556 Thomas Cranmer, Henry VIII and Edward VI's Protestant Archbishop of Canterbury, burned at the stake for opposing Mary.

1558 The English lose Calais (in France) to the French people. Mary unpopular for this and for her marriage to the Catholic Philip II of Spain. Luckily she dies before she is overthrown!

1558 – reign of Elizabeth I

1564 William Shakespeare born.
1567 Mary Queen of Scots thrown off her throne. She flees to England a year later.
1568 England and Spain begin to argue over control of the oceans.

1577 Francis Drake begins his voyage round the world – returns in 1580.
1587 Mary Queen of Scots executed.
1588 The Spanish Armada tries to invade England but is defeated.
1601 The Earl of Essex rebels against Elizabeth and is executed.

1603

End of Terrible Tudors – in come the Slimy Stuarts.

Kett's Rebellion

In Norfolk, 1549, the problem was too many sheep and too few jobs. The grumbles grew into a revolt. The revolting Norfolk men were led by the most revolting Robert Kett – a local landowner. But Robert's rebels grew hungry and weak. Edward VI sent the Earl of Warwick to deal with them. The Earl cut the rebels to pieces... but they weren't as cut up as Robert Kett might have been. He was sentenced to...

...be dragged to Tyburn, where he is to be hung and whilst still alive his entrails taken out and burned before him, his head cut off and his body cut into four pieces.

As it happened, Robert was taken to Norfolk Castle and hung in chains over the battlements.

Terrible Tudor life and death

Life begins at 40

Would **you** like to have lived in Tudor times? A 1980 school history book said... *All in all the Elizabethan Age was an extremely exciting time to be alive.* But this is a *Horrible History* book. You make up your own mind about how "exciting" it was when you have the real facts. For example... You probably know a lot of people who are 40 years old, or older. But would you have known as many in Tudor times?

Imagine that ten children were born on a particular day in a Tudor town. How many do you think would still be alive to celebrate their 40th birthdays?

a) 6   b) 9   c) 1   d) 4

Answer: c) On average, only one person in ten lived to the age of 40. Many died in childhood – the first year was the most dangerous of your life.

Why were Tudor times so unhealthy? Perhaps these will help you understand...

Half a dozen filthy facts

1 Open sewers ran through the streets and carried diseases.
2 Toilets were little more than a hole in the ground outside the back door.

3 Water came from village pumps. These often took the water from a local river, and that river was full of the filth from the town.

4 Country people made their own medicines from herbs, or went to an "apothecary". People still use herbal cures today ... but would you take one from a Tudor apothecary who didn't know the importance of washing their hands before handling your medicine?

5 A popular cure for illness was "blood-letting". Most people believed that too much blood made you ill. All you had to do was lose some and you'd feel better. Where could you go to lose some blood? The local barber. (He had a part-time job as a surgeon when he wasn't cutting hair!) Sometimes the barber would make a deep cut; other times a scratch was made, followed by a heated cup over the wound to "suck" the blood out.

6 Some doctors used slimy, blood-sucking creatures called leeches to suck blood out of the patient. (And some doctors today still use leeches to cure certain blood diseases!)

Doctor, doctor...!

If you were a doctor in Tudor times, what cures would you suggest for illnesses?

Here are ten illnesses - and ten Tudor cures. Match the cure to the illness...

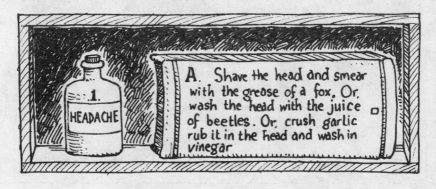

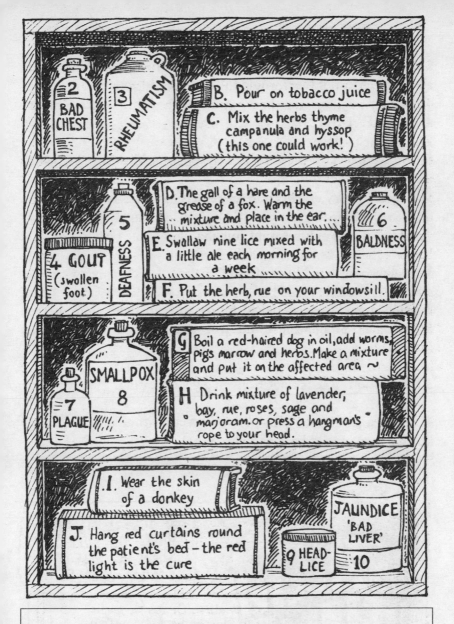

2 BAD CHEST

3 RHEUMATISM

B. Pour on tobacco juice

C. Mix the herbs thyme campanula and hyssop (this one could work!)

D. The gall of a hare and the grease of a fox. Warm the mixture and place in the ear.....

E. Swallow nine lice mixed with a little ale each morning for a week

F. Put the herb, rue on your windowsill.

4 GOUT (swollen foot)

5 DEAFNESS

6 BALDNESS

G. Boil a red-haired dog in oil, add worms, pigs marrow and herbs. Make a mixture and put it on the affected area ~

H. Drink mixture of lavender, bay, rue, roses, sage and marjoram. or press a hangman's rope to your head.

7 PLAGUE

SMALLPOX 8

I. Wear the skin of a donkey

J. Hang red curtains round the patient's bed – the red light is the cure

9 HEAD-LICE

JAUNDICE 'BAD LIVER' 10

Answers: 1=H 2=C 3=I 4=G 5=D 6=A 7=F 8=J 9=B 10=E

23

How did you do, Doctor? It wouldn't really matter if you got them all wrong. Most of them wouldn't have worked anyway!

Patient, patient…!

If you were sick in those extremely exciting Tudor times, which would you rather do?
Feel sick… or try one of these extremely exciting Tudor cures?

Ten cures you wouldn't want to try…

1 Swallow powdered human skull.

2 Eat live spiders (covered in butter to help them slide down a little easier). Swallowing young frogs was suggested as a cure for asthma.

3 Fustigation – the patient is given a good beating.

4 Throw a stone over your house – but the stone must first have killed a man, a wild boar or a she-bear.

OF COURSE IT'S BIG.. HAVE YOU EVER SEEN THE SIZE OF A SHE-BEAR?

5 Eat the scrapings from the skull of an executed criminal.

6 Eat bone-marrow mixed with sweat.

7 Sniff sneezing-powder to clear the head.

8 Have burning hot plasters placed on the body to raise blisters.

9 Mix the blood from a black cat's tail with cream, then drink it.

10 Place half a newly-killed pigeon on plague sores.

Nowadays we know that the dreadful plagues were carried by fleas. The Tudors didn't know about the disease they carried. Still, they weren't keen on fleas because they bit and made you itch. They had a cure you might like to try if you ever have them in your bedroom...

First, to gather all the fleas of thy chamber into one place, cover a staff with the grease of a fox or a hedgehog. Lay the staff in thy chamber and it shall gather all the fleas to it. Also, fill a dish with goat's blood and put it by the bed and all the fleas will come to it.

DON'T SLURP!

Fleas love to bite humans to get at their blood. They might well dash off to a whole dish of goat's blood!

Terrible Tudor schools

Parents, grandparents, teachers and other old fogeys ... they all do it. They all talk about "The Good Old Days". Then they go on to talk about how terrible it was in school. They say things like... When I was a young lad/lass/goldfish just knee-high to a grasshopper/grass hut/grass skirt schools were schools. You kids have it easy these days. We used to get a caning/whipping/sweet if we as much as opened our mouth/eyes/door. We had 6/12/25 hours of homework every night and we were kept in detention/prison/vinegar until we did it. They were the best days of our lives!"

If they think **their** schools were tough it's as well they didn't go to school in Tudor times. (Or maybe they did and they're lying when they tell you they're only 39.) If they had they would know that...

1 Most village children didn't go to school. A few might attend a "Dame" school run by a local dame (woman).

2 Children rarely had books. They may have had "Horn" books, though. These were pieces of wood the shape and size of a table-tennis bat. On one side was a printed page with the alphabet and perhaps, the Lord's Prayer. The other side was blank and could be used to practise writing.

`HORN' BOOK FOR SHORTSIGHTED PUPILS

3 Richer children could be sent away to school. At first, the monks in the monasteries ran most of the schools, known as choir schools. Henry VIII closed the monasteries because they were run by the Catholic Church. He started a new church, the Church of England, but he lost the schools in the process, and was left with

only a handful of grammar schools. He had to encourage new ones to be set up, but in fact only 20 more grammar schools were established during his reign. So much for education!

How does your school compare with a Tudor school? Check out these Tudor school rules and decide…

What to expect at school

Timetable

School lessons went on from dawn till sunset with a break for school dinners.

(If you lived a long way from school, you'd have to get up in the dark to allow time for walking. The roads were muddy, cold and dangerous on the short winter days.)

~ SCHOOL RULES ~

No scholar shall wear a dagger or any other weapon. They shall not bring to school any stick or bat, only their meat knife.

Manchester Grammar School 1528
It is ordered that for every oath or rude word spoken, in the school or elsewhere, the scholar shall have three strokes of the cane.

Oundle School 1566
Scholars shall not go to taverns or ale-houses and must not play unlawful games such as cards, dice or the like.

Hawkshead School 1585
Punishment for losing your school cap . . . a beating
Punishment for making fun of another pupil . . . a beating.

THAT'S A MEAT KNIFE? #6!!! HA HA HA

School swots

Working hard at school was not always popular with the upper-class parent.

One father said, *I'd rather see my son hanged than be a bookworm. It is a gentleman's life to hunt and to hawk. A gentleman should leave learning to clodhoppers.*

~ SCHOOL MEALS ~

Breakfast
Bread and butter and a little fruit

Lunch
Rye bread, salted meat and ale

Tea
Bread with dried fruit and nuts – fresh fruit in summer

Rules at meal times
1 Wear a cap to keep your hair out of your food.
2 Don't wipe your mouth with your hand or sleeve.
3 Don't let your sleeve drag in your food.
4 Don't lean on the table.
5 Don't pick your teeth with your pen-knife or your fork.
Punishment for breaking a rule . . . a beating.

WHERE'S MY CAP?

School teachers

Their job (in Westminster School at least) was to see that their pupils:

behave themselves properly in church and school as well as in games, that their faces and hands are washed, their heads combed, their hair and nails cut, their clothes and shoes kept clean so that no lice or dirt may infect themselves or their companions.

School punishments

Schoolmasters would often beat their pupils. Henry Peachum wrote,

I know one who in winter would, on a cold morning, whip his boys for no other reason than to warm himself up. Another beat them for swearing, and all the while he swore himself with horrible oaths.

But they weren't all so bad. The headmaster of Eton in 1531 was Nicholas Udall. He wrote the first English play that wasn't religious, and it was also the first comedy play.

School holidays

No long holidays. Schools would close for 16 days at Christmas and 12 days at Easter, but there were no summer holidays.

Lessons

A class might have as many as 60 pupils. Many hours were spent learning long passages from textbooks by heart. This not only kept them all quiet – it also saved having to buy books! Main subjects: Latin, Arithmetic, Divinity (Religious Study), English Literature.

School sports

A Shrove Tuesday custom was to take money to school, and with it the schoolmaster would buy a fighting cock. The master put a long string on the cock and tied it to a post. Boys would then take turns at throwing a stick at the cock. If a boy hit then the cock became his - if every boy hit then the cock belonged to the schoolmaster.

School equipment

Pupils had to write with quill pens made from feathers. These would have to be sharpened with a knife nearly every day. The small knife used was called a pen-knife - and we can still buy "penknives" today ... even if we don't sharpen our ballpoints with them.

If you'd really like to know what it was like to write with a quill pen then you could try making one.

You need

1. A strong feather – goose quill is best, but turkey or any other strong feather will do.
2. A pen-knife – if you haven't a pen-knife then a Stanley knife will be just as good.
3. Tweezers.
4. Ink.

And an adult to make sure you don't get chopped fingers on the table!

How to make it

1. Shorten the feather to about 20cm.
2. Strip off all the barbs (the feathery part) from the shaft.

(Yes, I know! In all the pictures you've seen the writers appear to be writing with feathers. They hardly ever did they only used the shaft and threw the rest away. Honest!)

3 Cut the bottom of the shaft off with your pen-knife (Figure 1).

4 Shape the bottom of the shaft as in Figure 2. Take out the core with tweezers.

5 Make a slit at the end of the nib about 5mm long (Figure 3).

6 Trim the end of the shaft again, this time at an angle. (Figure 4 shows the angle for a right-handed writer)

7 Dip the quill in ink. Try writing an alphabet.

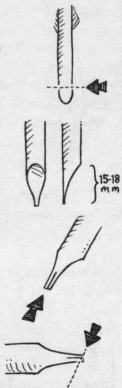

15-18 mm

ABCDE ⌐ Gh 👁 JK l m

Test your teacher on Tudors

Here are a couple of facts your teacher (or parents or friends) may think they know. Perhaps you'll catch them out if you ask...

1 The first post

You: Please, Miss! (or Sir, or Fatface) Who had the first postal service in this country?

Teacher: I'm glad you asked me that...

(Teachers are always glad when you ask them something – it makes them think you are interested.)

    ...Of course, everybody knows that the famous Victorian, Rowland Hill, invented the postal service.

You: (with a sigh) But my book on the Terrible Tudors says the first postal service was invented in the reign of Elizabeth the First!

Then go on to quote these facts...

Rowland Hill created the Penny Post and postage stamps, not the postal service. Tudor Guilds and universities had private postal services. The government was worried about spies sending messages out of the country this way. So they insisted that a service under The Master of Posts should carry all letters sent outside England – that way they could read them if they suspected something!

2 A miss is as good as a mile

You: Please, Sir! (or Miss, or Fairy-features) If you asked Henry VIII how many yards there are in a mile, what would he say?

Teacher: I'm glad you asked me that... He would say 1,760 yards, of course.

You: That's not what my book on the Terrible Tudors says. It says that if you asked Henry VIII how many yards there are in a mile he would say, "It depends where you are."

Teacher: Eh!?!

You: (Explain) It wasn't till Queen Elizabeth's reign that a mile was fixed at 1,760 yards. Before that it depended on where you lived.

LONDON MILE = 5,000 yards
ENGLISH MILE = 6,610 yards
WELSH MILE - about 4 modern miles
IRISH MILE = 2,240 yards
SCOTTISH MILE = 1,976 yards

I THOUGHT YOU MIGHT HAVE KNOWN THAT, MISS!

Then count your lucky stars that you aren't in school in Tudor times!

Tudor crime ... and terrible punishments

In Britain in 1992 crime was the fourth largest "business" in the country - people on both sides of the law made 14 billion pounds. In Tudor times it must have been as bad, with more than 10,000 homeless beggars on the city streets. Many were simply rogues who tricked, cheated and stole from kindhearted people who thought they were helping the poor. Yes, there were more crimes in those days ... and more punishments. Some of them seem incredible today.

Thieving

Humphrey Lisle's story – Newcastle, 1528

Humphrey Lisle must have been worried. Dead worried.

He knew the English laws of 1528: steal up to eleven pence and you went to prison. Steal twelve pence (one shilling) or more... and you could be hanged. Humphrey had been one of a gang of Scottish raiders who'd stolen much more than twelve pence. One of the charges against Humphrey said that he...

at Gosforth, a mile from Newcastle, took prisoner twenty-seven people passing by in the High Street, from whom he took 26 shillings and 8 pence. He ransomed all but seven whom he kept for a while as slaves in Scotland.

Stealing twenty-seven shillings! Kidnapping! Slavery! Humphrey and the gang had been caught and locked up in Newcastle jail. The gang were the worst villains in the North and now they were safely in chains in prison.

They were still in chains when they went to court. One by one the judge sentenced them to death. Humphrey's father was sentenced to death first. Then it was Humphrey's turn.

"You admit to all the charges against you?" the judge asked.

"Aye, sir," Humphrey answered.

"But I am not going to sentence you to death," the judge went on.

A gasp of surprise went around the court. They had been looking forward to seeing Humphrey's head stuck on a pole on the town walls. It was just what he deserved, wasn't it? The Newcastle people couldn't understand why the judge spared Humphrey's life.

Can you give a reason for the judge sparing Humphrey s life?
Was it because…

1 Humphrey had friends outside who threatened to have the judge killed?
2 Humphrey was very rich and offered the judge a lot of money?
3 Humphrey was the youngest in the gang and the judge wanted to give him a second chance?
4 Humphrey was Scottish and so was the judge?

Answer: 3. Humphrey Lisle was just twelve years old when he joined the gang that stole, burned, murdered and kidnapped its way through the north. The judge took pity on him. Within a few years Humphrey Lisle was working for the English … helping to catch Scottish raiders!

Believing is a crime

Tudor people were very concerned with religion. It was important to the kings and queens, to the people and to the law. Catholicism was the religion of England and most European countries until the 16th century.

But the invention of the printing press in the 15th century meant that more and more people had access to the Bible and were beginning to question the wisdom of priests. Ordinary folk were expected to believe all sorts of things, and were encouraged to buy "relics". These were things like bits of old bone and hair that some priests said belonged to saints. Yuk! Anyway, all this led to people wanting change within the Church.

And some kings and queens, who wanted absolute power without interference from Catholic leaders, were only too happy to encourage this change, which was known as the Reformation. The "reformists" were generally known as Protestants. There was a lot of hatred between the Catholics and the Protestants.

Catholics wanted...

The Pope as head of the church – services in Latin – churches decorated with paintings and statues.

Protestants wanted...

No Pope – services in English – plain churches.

Often, the hatred between them was terribly deadly...

Margaret Clitheroe's story – York, 1586

Margaret Clitheroe was a Catholic. In the days of Elizabeth I that was not a safe thing to be. But a lot of Catholics kept their religion and stayed secure by playing safe. They went to the Church of England services as the law said they had to. They kept their Catholic beliefs quietly to themselves.

But Margaret Clitheroe was not that sort of woman. She was a "recusant" - she refused to go to a protestant church.

Her husband, John, was a rich butcher in the city of York. "Margaret," he sighed, "the officers of the law cannot ignore you any longer. They will take you to court and fine you. Come to church with me today. It can't do you any harm!"

But Margaret was stubborn. "No, John." He shook his head and left for church. He walked by Micklegate Bar, one of the main gates of York. The remains of executed Catholics were still hanging there, more grisly than anything on his butcher's stall. He shuddered and wished his wife would learn some sense.

He'd have been still more worried had he known that Margaret was doing more than just missing church. She was also hiding Catholic priests in their house. But not for much longer.

The officers had started questioning people who knew Margaret Clitheroe. They were trying to make a case against her. When they captured a young servant, that case was complete. They threatened him with a beating, so he told them everything they wanted to know- and more. He told them about hiding Catholic priests. He showed them the hiding places.

On Monday 10 March 1586 they came for Margaret. She stood silent before Judge Clinch. "Have you anything to say, Margaret Clitheroe?" the judge asked.

Margaret said nothing. She knew that if she answered the charges then the law would call witnesses against her. The best witnesses would be her own children. If the children didn't want to talk then they would be tortured until they betrayed their mother.

The judge nodded. "Of course, the punishment for refusing to stand trial is Death By Crushing, do you know that, Mrs Clitheroe?"

Margaret knew. She had heard about "death by crushing". The accused was laid on the ground, face up. A sharp stone, about the size of a man's fist, was placed under the back. The face was covered with a handkerchief. A heavy door was laid on the accused. Large stones were placed on the door until the accused was crushed to death.

Margaret had to choose. Did she...

1 Remain silent and face death by crushing?
2 Stand trial and have her children as witnesses against her?

The good – the Justice of the Peace

Which would you rather do:
1 live by the laws of the Tudor land?
2 break the laws of Tudor times?
3 have the job of enforcing Tudor laws?
The people who had the job of enforcing the laws were usually Justices of the Peace. (We still have them today but they don't have so much power.)
If you were a Justice of the Peace you would have to...
1 stop riots
2 look after the building of roads, bridges, jails and poorhouses
3 decide how much local workers could be paid
4 report people who didn't go to church
5 be in charge of the whipping of beggars
6 check on the local alehouses.

RIOTS ?
ROADS ?
WORKERS ?
REPORTS ?
WHIPPING ?
CHECKING ?
OH DEAR

But your main job would be to judge cases in your local court. Would you know all of the curious laws? Try to match the law to the crime first…

LAW	CRIME
1 Archery	A. More than 3 people making trouble together.
2 Unlawful games	B. Quarrelling
3 Rescue	C. Playing bowls, cards or dice on a holy day.
4 Barratry	D. Stirring up trouble for the king or queen.
5 Inmate	E. Refusing to go to church.
6 Riot	F Not going to regular weapons practices.
7 Recusance	G. Taking a person or an animal by force.
8 Sedition	H Letting part of your house to someone without a job.

Answers: 1 = F 2 = C 3 = G 4 = B 5 = H 6 = A 7 = E 8 = D

Now test your teacher! Bet they can't get more than 5!

Try your own court case

Now that you know the laws you can try a few cases. If you were a judge you'd have a lot of different punishments you could deal out. On the right is a list of the punishments – on the left is a list of crimes. Can you match the punishment to the crime?

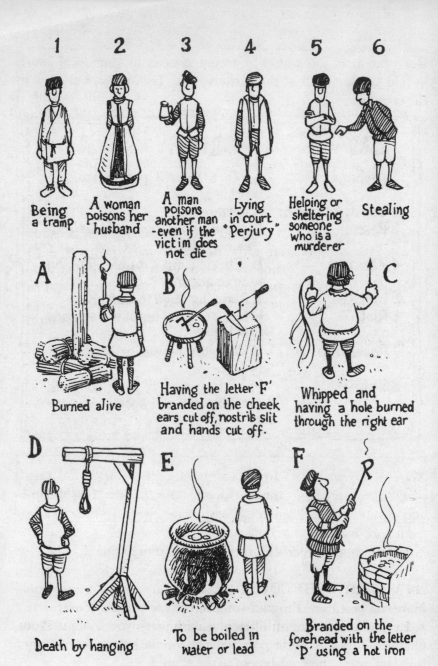

1 Being a tramp

2 A woman poisons her husband

3 A man poisons another man - even if the victim does not die

4 Lying in court "Perjury"

5 Helping or sheltering someone who is a murderer

6 Stealing

A Burned alive

B Having the letter 'F' branded on the cheek ears cut off, nostrils slit and hands cut off.

C Whipped and having a hole burned through the right ear

D Death by hanging

E To be boiled in water or lead

F Branded on the forehead with the letter 'P' using a hot iron

Rotten rules

There wasn't a lot of freedom in Tudor times. Henry VIII passed a law telling people how much money they could earn... a craftsman could make just six pence a day in 1514. For that you had to work from five o'clock in the morning till six o'clock at night from March to September. In the winter months you would just(!) work from sunrise till sunset with one hour for breakfast and one-and-a-half hours for lunch. A servant could earn 160 pence a year – but a woman-servant could only earn 120 pence!

Elizabeth I passed a law telling people they could only wear clothes the queen thought suitable. And you had to wear a woollen hat on Sunday – or else! (That was so the English wool trade could make big profits and pay lots of lovely taxes to the queen!)

Even if you stayed out of trouble with the Justices of the Peace, you still had to worry about work. Most workers belonged to a Guild - a sort of union for their trade. There were guilds for goldsmiths and weavers and carpenters and shoemakers and so on. And every guild had its own laws. Heaven help you if you broke a guild law! It was worst for the young people who joined the guilds for the first time - the "Apprentices". Here are just a few of the rules they had to obey...

Apprentices must not use any music by night or day in the streets. Neither shall they wear their hair long, nor hair at their ears like ruffians (1603).

And the punishment for long hair? A basin was put over the boy's head and the hair chopped off in a straight line. He was then sent to prison for ten days! (We still call a straight-cut fringe a pudding-basin cut.)

Apprentices were in trouble in 1554 for *playing cards, drinking, dancing and embracing women,* and their appearance was so grand and flashy they were banned from wearing silk-lined clothes, from having beards or from carrying daggers.

In a Weaver's Guild meeting (1527) you had to behave or...
Any brother misbehaving at meetings to be fined six pounds of wax.
(Wax was valuable, as it was needed for candles)

...but worse, such was the hatred between the Scots and the English, that
Any brother calling another "Scot" to be fined six shillings and eight pence.
...that's twelve weeks' wages!

The Tudor law

The rich nobles had been a "law unto themselves" – the Tudors put a stop to that. They were no longer allowed to keep private armies.

Bribing of judges and juries had been common the Tudors stopped that ... well, *mostly!*

The rich had been able to dodge the law – now rich lawbreakers could be taken before the Tudor kings' "Star Chamber". Punishments usually took the form of big fines.

Terrible Tudor detectives

The Tudors had no policemen. They did take it in turns to be "constables" and check on some of the laws. They also had local "detectives" called "cunning men", or "wizards". The village Cunning Man might use good magic to cure illnesses and tell fortunes. But he also had a use as a detective.

One of his methods of finding out a guilty person was to make a list of all the "suspects". Each suspect's name was written on a piece of paper. Each piece of paper was wrapped in a clay ball. The clay balls were dropped into a bucket of water. The one that unrolled first had the name of the guilty person on it! That's if the water didn't wash the ink off first!

The bad – the criminals

If you weren't afraid of being caught – or if you were very desperate for money and food to stay alive – you might become a criminal.

What sort would you like to be? A prigger of prancers? A dummerer? Or, maybe a ruffler?

What do you mean, you don't understand? If you're going to become a Tudor criminal you need to learn the language.

-ROGUES-
DICTIONARY

beak   **walking mort**

beak – magistrate
boozing ken - ale house
a bung – a purse
chats – gallows
a cony – an easy victim
cove – man
couch a hogshead –
   go to sleep
draw – pick a pocket
filchman – strong pole for
   walking or hitting
a foist – a pickpocket
glaziers – eyes
greenman's – fields

ken – house
lift – rob a shop
mort – woman
nab – head
peck – food
prancer – horse
prig – steal
a snap – a share of loot
stamps – legs
stow you – shut up
three trees with a ladder
  – gallows
walking mort – woman
  tramp

THAT HISTORY TEACHER'S A WALKING MORT. I WISH SHE'D STOW HER SO I CAN COUCH A HOGSHEAD. IN FACT IF YOU KEEP YOUR GLAZIERS ON HER I MAY JUST PRIG A NAP!

Become a terrible criminal!

Learn some of the language yourself – add new words of your own – and baffle everyone around you! Once you've grasped the language, you are almost ready to learn some tricks of the trade. But first you'll need a name – to protect your true identity. You need to change your name.

In Tudor times a few villains' nick-names were...
Olli Compoli,
Dimber Damber,
Black Will,
Shagbag.

Women were...
the White Ewe,
the Lamb, and so on.

What would you call yourself? You can make up your own name.

The Wickedness – the crimes

What villainy would you like to be involved in? You could try being one of these...

An Autem Mort – a woman who steals clothes off washing lines.

A Hooker (or Angler) – a thief who uses a long pole with a hook on the end to "lift" other people's property.

They carry with them a staff five or six feet long, in which, within one inch of the top, is a little hole bored. In this hole they put an iron hook. With the same they will pluck unto them anything that they may reach. The hook, in the daytime, they hide and is never taken out until they come to the place where they do their stealing. They will lean upon their staff to hide the hole while they talk to you.

A Prigger of Prancers - a horse stealer.

A Ruffler - a beggar who tries to squeeze money out of you with a sad story about how he fought and was wounded in the wars.

A Dummerer - a beggar who tries to win sympathy by acting both deaf and dumb.

An Abram Man - a beggar who pretends to be mad, wears ragged clothes, dances around and talks nonsense… Try saying, "Please let me have some of your sheep's feathers to make a bed!"

Highway Robber - seems to be a beggar when he stops you on a quiet road, but when you take your purse out he snatches it and may throw you off your horse and take that too.

Palliard - a beggar with dreadful sores. Could be genuine disease, but (more often) they'd be faked.

They take crowfoot, spearwort and salt and lay them upon the part of the body they desire to make sore. The skin by this means being irritated, they first clasp to a linen cloth till it sticks fast. When the cloth is plucked off the raw flesh has rat poison thrown upon it to make it look ugly. They then cast over that a cloth which is always bloody and filthy. They do this so often that in the end they feel no pain, nor do they want to have it healed. They travel from fair to fair and from market to market. They are able to live by begging and sometimes have about them five or six pounds altogether.

A Doxy (or walking Mort) - a woman tramp.
On her back she carries a great pack in which she has all the things she steals. Her skill sometimes is to tell fortunes or to help cure the diseases of women and children. As she walks she knits and wears in her hat a needle with a thread in it. If any poultry be near she feeds them with bread on the hook and has the thread tied to the hook. The chicken, swallowing this, is choked and hidden under the cloak. Chickens, clothing or anything that is worth the catching comes into her net.

50

A Cutpurse - purses were small coin-bags hanging from the belt. If you couldn't "foist" the purse (dip in and pick the money out) then you would have to "nip" it (cut the purse off).

A good foist must have three qualities that a good surgeon should have and they are an eagle's eye (to spy out where the bung lies) a lady's hand (to be little and nimble) and a lion's heart.

Terrible Shakespeare

Terrible Shakespeare has been torturing school pupils for hundreds of years!

It isn't his fault, though. Teachers were taught by teachers who were taught by teachers who were taught, "Shakespeare is the greatest poet and playwright ever. You are going to listen to him even if it bores the knickers off you! Now, sit still and stop yawning!"

In fact, Shakespeare didn't write for school pupils to read his plays and study every last word. He wrote the plays to be **acted** and **enjoyed** ... so act them and **enjoy** them.

You can start by practising a few Terrible Shakespeare insults. Go up to the nearest nasty teacher (or policeman or parent or priest) and try one of these insults on them. Then, just before they mince you into hamster food, say, "Oh, but Sir (or Miss or Constable or Your Holiness), I was just practising my Shakespeare. He's the greatest poet and playwright ever." Smile sweetly and add, "And you do want me to study Shakespeare, don't you?"

Here goes…

(Never mind what they mean ... just enjoy saying them aloud!)
Feeling really brave now, are you? Then try...

Feeling suicidal? Then go up to the man with the biggest ears you can find and say Shakespeare's nastiest insult...

The Tudor Theatre

Being an actor in Tudor times was just a little different from today. For a start there were no actresses in Tudor theatre. All the women's parts were played by boys. Often the women in Shakespeare's plays disguised themselves as boys, so you'd have a boy pretending to be a woman pretending to be a boy. Nowadays women play the women's parts so you have women pretending to be boys pretending to be women pretending to be boys!

Get it? Oh, never mind.

Shakespeare's theatres were all open air stages. The audience would sit around three sides of the stage - if you were poor you would have to stand ... and Shakespeare's play, Hamlet, went on for over three hours!

His plays are often performed on Elizabethan style stages today. You can see them in Shakespeare's birthplace, Stratford-upon-Avon.

Most of the audience couldn't read so it was no use putting up posters. The signal that a play was going to start was a cannon fired from the top of the theatre roof. Unfortunately, one such cannon shot set fire to the thatched roof of one of Shakespeare's theatres and burned it to the ground.

ARE YOU THE GIRL WHO'S A BOY WHO'S A GIRL WHO'S A BOY OR AM I ?

Dramatic facts about William Shakespeare

1 Shakespeare was born on St George's Day (23 April) in 1564. He died in 1616 ... on 23 April, St George's day! That must have put a bit of a damper on his 52nd birthday party.

2 Shakespeare chose the epitaph for his own gravestone. It says...

Some people think there may be new and priceless Shakespeare plays buried in the tomb ... but no one has risked the curse of digging it up.

3 In his will he left his wife his *second-best bed, with the furniture.*

4 Some people have tried to rewrite Shakespeare's plays. In the eighteenth century, a man called Nahum Tate rewrote many. He took the sad and gory tragedies (like *Macbeth*) and gave them happy endings just because people prefer them!

5 Actors are very superstitious people. Their greatest superstition is that *Macbeth* is an unlucky play. Never, never say a line from the play (unless you are acting, it of course). Don't even say the title ... call it "The Scottish Play" if you have to call it anything. And if you do act in it then watch out

... the "Macbeth Curse" may get you. This is the terrible bad luck that seems to happen to every production accident, illness and even death. Many actors will swear that it's true because it's happened to someone they know.

6 The most dramatic fact of all? Perhaps William Shakespeare didn't write William Shakespeare's plays! Some very serious teachers believe that the man called Shakespeare could not have written plays. Why not? Because...

a William Shakespeare's father could not read or write, nor could Shakespeare's children

b the few signatures of Shakespeare that remain show a very poor scrawl

c William Shakespeare was known in Stratford as a businessman, not a writer

d there are no manuscripts of Shakespeare's plays in the man's own handwriting – there are lots from other writers of the time

e he left no manuscripts in his will and no copies of his plays are mentioned as being in his house

f a monument put up in Stratford church 15 years after he died show his hands resting on a sack (a sign of a tradesman) not a pen

g there is no evidence, apart from the name, to link the Stratford actor/businessman with the playwright.

7 Professor Calvin Hoffman has studied the language used by writers. If you look at the way a writer uses words of a certain number of letters then you can recognise his writing. Every writer is different – just as everyone has different fingerprints. Yet Shakespeare's writing "fingerprint" is identical to that of another leading Elizabethan playwright, Christopher Marlowe.

So, did Marlowe write the plays and put William Shakespeare's name on them? Is it possible? No. Because, six months before Shakespeare's first publication, Christopher Marlowe is said to have been murdered.

Or was he…

Terrible Tudor mystery

The murder of Christopher Marlowe?

The murderer's story

Date: Wednesday 30 May 1593
Place: Eleanor Bull's Tavern, Deptford, London

Mrs Bull mopped at the spilt ale on the table with a dirty cloth. It dribbled onto the sawdust on the floor. Suddenly, three men clattered down the stairs and fell into the room. Three of the men she'd let the upstairs room to.

"Mrs Bull! Oh, Mrs Bull!" the skinny Ingram Frizer gasped as he clutched at his head.

"What's wrong?" the woman snapped. Frizer was a well-known trickster who'd tried to cheat her more than once.

The man took his hand away from his head. It was soaked in blood. "Murder!" he said hoarsely.

"Sit down," she said briskly. Frizer's two friends, Skeres and Poley, helped him to a bench. The woman mopped at the head wounds with her ale cloth and sniffed. "Not murder, Mr Frizer, just a couple of two-inch cuts. You'll not die. Who did it?"

"Marlowe," the man moaned, "Christopher Marlowe."

The woman looked at the stairs and snatched a bread knife from the bar. "Roaming around stabbing people, is he?"

The wounded man shook his head slowly. "Not any more, he's not."

Mrs Bull relaxed. "You overpowered him, then?"

Frizer's voice dropped to a whisper. "I killed him!"

The landlady grabbed the man by the collar and marched him

towards the stairs. "Let's have a look at poor Mr Marlowe, shall we?" she demanded. Frizer couldn't argue. Skeres and Poley lurked behind as she threw open the door.

The body lay on the floor. One lifeless eye stared at the ceiling. The other was covered in blood from a neat wound just above it.

"I knew you were trouble, you three," the woman moaned. "That Mr Marlowe seemed such a nice young man. What happened?" She looked closely at the body and shook her head. "Doesn't look a bad enough wound to kill a man that quick," she muttered.

Frizer swayed and let himself fall onto the bed.

"He was lying here, on this bed. We had our backs to him, didn't we Poley?"

Poley nodded. The local men said Poley made his money from spying. "Our backs to him," he said.

"Suddenly he jumped up from the bed, snatched my dagger and started stabbing at my head!" Frizer groaned. "I had Skeres on one side of me and Poley on the other. I couldn't get out of the way, could I?"

"He couldn't!" Skeres agreed. Everybody knew that Skeres was a cutpurse and a robber.

"If he attacked you from behind he could have killed you easily, not just scratched your scalp, Mr Frizer," the landlady argued.

"I moved," the man said lamely.

"Then he stabbed himself in the eye, did he?" Mrs Bull asked with a sneer.

"No!" Poley cried. "I managed to get the dagger from him. We struggled. It went into his eye by accident."

"A strange sort of accident. Doesn't look the sort of wound you'd get from a scuffle. Looks more like he was lying on his back when the knife went in," the woman said carefully.

The three men looked at each other nervously.

"Just one of those things," Poley mumbled.

"So what were you arguing about?" the landlady asked. "I didn't hear any argument."

"About the bill," Frizer said quickly.

"And why didn't your two friends help?" she asked suspiciously.

"It wasn't our argument," Skeres shrugged.

"You'll hang for this, Mr Frizer," Mrs Bull said contentedly.

Frizer looked up slowly from the bed. A curious smile came over his face. "Oh no I won't, Mrs Bull. Oh, no I won't."

And he didn't.

A strange sort of accident indeed. But the jury decided that was just what it was. You might have decided the same if you'd been on the jury. But looking back over 400 years you have a few more facts to go on. Here they are…

The powerful and important Sir Thomas Walsingham was a friend of all of the men and could have helped them get away with a plan such as this. Christopher Marlowe was certainly his closest friend.

Marlowe was in deep trouble at the time of his "death". His friend, Thomas Kyd, had just been arrested for having writings which said that Jesus was not the Son of God. The punishment for this was death. Kyd said the writings belonged to Christopher Marlowe! (It did Kyd no good – he died after being "put to torture" in prison a year later.)

Frizer went back to work for Walsingham after he had been tried for the murder of Marlowe.

So what happened in Mrs Bull's tavern that day? If you don't believe Frizer's story, here are two other stories that fit the facts…

The execution theory

Marlowe had been careless. He'd left those writings in Kyd's room. Marlowe would be arrested and executed. Marlowe was as good as dead.

Kyd had accused Marlowe. But if Marlowe went to court he might have brought Sir Thomas Walsingham into all this. That would never have done.

Sir Thomas called his three loyal cut-throats to him. He gave them their orders, "Kill Marlowe and I will reward you well. Make it look like an accident and I'll use all my power to make sure the court lets you go free."

The three agreed to meet Marlowe in the tavern. As the playwright lay drunk on the bed, Skeres and Poley held him down while Frizer pushed the knife into his eye. Skeres or Poley then gave Frizer a couple of cuts on the head to back up their story of a fight.

Or…

The escape theory

Sir Thomas Walsingham was a great friend of Christopher Marlowe. He heard that Marlowe was about to be arrested for a crime that could lead to his execution. Sir Thomas wanted to protect his friend.

He called the four men to his house and told them of his plan. Marlowe must leave the country as soon as possible. As soon as he was safe abroad the other three must take a stranger to Mrs Bull's tavern and kill him.

After the murder, Frizer must confess. Say it was a fight and that "Marlowe" had been killed. When a man owns up to murder, the constables are interested in establishing the killer – not the identity of the victim. The stranger was buried in a grave named "Christopher Marlowe" and the real Marlowe was safe.

Of course, the real Marlowe was a successful playwright. Imagine Marlowe wants to go on writing plays. So he does. He sends them to Walsingham. Walsingham gives them to an actor. An ambitious young man who happily signs his own name to Marlowe's plays.

He signs them, "William Shakespeare".

Possible? What do you think? Remember, history is not always simple or straightforward. In cases like this historians make up their own minds from the facts that they have. So, you can be an historical "police officer". In cases like this, what you think is as good as what another historian might think.

Terrible Tudor kings and queens

Things they try to teach you

Henry VII
Henry Tudor became King Henry VII after defeating Richard III at the Battle of Bosworth Field.

True, but Henry had a lot of help from other lords, including one (Stanley) who might have fought for Richard. When he chose to fight for Henry he won the battle for him and changed the course of English history!

Richard III was a grotesque man – he was hunch-backed and cruel.

Richard was no crueller than most rulers of the time. The stories of his twisted body were added to by Henry Tudor's history writers. England was full of cruel lords – only the cruellest of all could hope to control them and that was Henry Tudor!

Richard III died in battle crying, 'A horse, A horse! My kingdom for a horse!'

That's extremely unlikely! The lines were written by William Shakespeare 100 years after the battle in his play *Richard III*.

When Richard was killed in the Battle of Bosworth, his crown was found hanging from a thorn-bush and Henry was handed it on the battlefield.

It's a nice image, but not necessarily true.

Henry was fighting Richard III in the so-called 'Wars of the Roses'. Richard was fighting under the White Rose of the York Family emblem and Henry Tudor under the Red Rose of the Lancaster Family emblem.

In fact Richard fought under the banner of a Boar, while Henry Tudor battled under the Dragon symbol of his native Wales. The white rose/red-rose idea was thought up by Henry Tudor years later.

 Henry VII was a clever man and a wise ruler.

True – but he was also a man of the Middle Ages with some strange ideas. The story goes that he'd heard that the Mastiff type of dog was the only one brave enough to attack a lion. But the symbol on the English flag was a lion – so he ordered all the Mastiff dogs in England to be destroyed! (Richard was just as superstitious. Freak weather conditions meant that there appeared to be two suns shining in the sky before the battle of Bosworth Field. Richard took this as a sign that he was going to lose ... and he did.)

 Henry VII made England a wealthy country by carefully handling its money.

True – but Henry was so careful with money most people would call him very, very mean! And he wanted lots of money so that he didn't have to beg Parliament for it – which meant that he didn't have to take any notice of what Parliament said.

 All the money Henry VII saved for England was spent by his son, Henry VIII...
> True!

Things you could try to teach them!

Henry VIII

• Henry is famous for his six wives. But, did you know that in just one year (1536) his first wife (Catherine) died, his second (Anne Boleyn) was beheaded and he married his third (Jane Seymour).

• Henry was fond of cock-fighting so he had his own cock-fighting pit built at Whitehall in London. There are different battles fought on the site today - it is number 10 Downing Street, the home of the Prime Minister!

• Henry was famous for his love of music. He composed many pieces and was a keen singer. He owned ten trombones, 14 trumpets, five bagpipes, 76 recorders and 78 flutes. It is said he composed the tune, *Greensleeves*.

• Henry was a show-off. He organised a great tournament near Calais in France, known as the *Field of the Cloth of Gold*. It seemed mainly a chance for him to display his own sporting talents. He is said to have tired out six horses while performing a thousand jumps ... *to the delight of everyone*.

• Henry was an expert archer. He used to have competitions with a hundred of his guards and often did well. At the *Field of the Cloth of Gold* in 1520 he amazed people by hitting the bulls-eye repeatedly at a distance of 220 metres.

• Henry fancied himself as a wrestler. At a wrestling contest at the *Field of the Cloth of Gold* he created a stir by challenging King Francis I of France with the words... Brother we will wrestle. Francis couldn't refuse even though Henry was taller and heavier. Francis used a French-style trip and won – the English thought this was cheating; the French probably thought it served big Henry right.

• Henry liked to play an indoor tennis game called "Paume". He didn't go to see his wife, Anne Boleyn, executed. He was playing tennis while she had her head chopped off. As soon as he was brought the news of Anne's death, he rushed off to see his next love, Jane Seymour.

I'M BEING TREATED IN A VERY BACKHAND MANNER

• Even hard Henry VIII had a heart. He needed a son to carry on the Tudor royal name. He was so furious when Anne Boleyn produced baby Elizabeth that he refused to go to the christening!
• Henry wanted to get rid of Anne Boleyn for giving him only a female child. Her other babies died. One of the things he accused her of was being a witch. He had some support from the Tudor people in this. Anne had been born with a sign of the devil on her ... she had six fingers on her left hand!
• Only his third wife, Jane Seymour, gave him the son he wanted - then she died a few days later. Of his six wives it was Jane Seymour he asked to be buried next to when he died.

• Henry agreed to marry Anne of Cleves after he was shown a picture of her. She turned out to be a bit uglier than the picture. Henry was so upset he accused the Dutch of sending him a horse instead of a princess. He called her the Flanders Mare and divorced her after just six months.

Elizabeth I - what they said about her

It's difficult to know what Elizabeth looked like because although there are a lot of portraits of her, she didn't pose for many of them. And if a picture displeased her then she would have it destroyed.

Many painters have done portraits of the queen but none has sufficiently shown her looks or charms. Therefore her majesty commands all manner of persons to stop doing portraits of her until a clever painter has finished one which all other painters can copy. Her majesty, in the meantime, forbids the showing of any portraits which are ugly until they are improved. Lord Cecil

So, will we ever know exactly what she looked like? Only from what people wrote about her. Could you draw her from the descriptions?

She is now about twenty-one years old; her figure and face are very handsome; she has such an air of dignified majesty that no one could ever doubt that she is a queen.

VENETIAN AMBASSADOR

She is now twenty-three years old; although her face is comely rather than handsome, she is tall and well-formed, with a good skin, although swarthy; she has fine eyes and, above all, a beautiful hand with which she makes display.

ANOTHER VENETIAN AMBASSADOR

> *Her hair was more reddish than yellow, curled naturally in appearance.*

SCOTTISH AMBASSADOR 1564

> *In her sixty-fifth year her face is oblong, fair, but wrinkled; her eyes small, yet black and pleasant; her nose a little hooked; her teeth black (a fault the English seem to suffer from because of their great use of sugar); she wore false hair, and that red; her hands were small, her fingers long and her height neither tall nor short; her air was stately, her manner of speaking mild and good-natured.*

GERMAN VISITOR 1598

> *When anyone speaks of her beauty she says she was never beautiful. Nevertheless, she speaks of her beauty as often as she can.*

de MAISSE FRENCH VISITOR 1597

Elizabeth did not want to have her rotten teeth removed. Perhaps she was afraid. To show her how easy and painless it was, the brave Bishop of London had one of his own teeth taken out while she watched.

What Elizabeth I said about herself

I know I have the body of a weak and feeble woman, but I have the heart and stomach of a king, and a king of England too. I think foul scorn that any prince of Europe shall dare to invade the borders of my realm.

SHE WOULDN'T WANT THE STOMACH OF HENRY VIII

Her speech to her troops as the Spanish Armada approached

A weak and feeble woman? That's not what writers of her time said. Elizabeth had a temper which everyone feared. William Davison, her unfortunate secretary, was just one who suffered: *She punched and kicked him and told him to get out of her sight.*

And...

She threw a slipper at Walsingham (her secretary) and hit him in the face, which is not an unusual thing for her to do as she is always behaving in such a rude manner as this.

And...

Once she sent a letter to the Earl of Essex which was so fierce that he fainted. He became so swelled up that all the buttons on his doublet broke away as though they had been cut with a knife.

What can we do about Mary?

In 1568 Mary Queen of Scots had to leave Scotland in a great hurry. She was suspected of being mixed up in the murder of her husband, and she was a Catholic. She also had a claim to the throne of England. She was a threat to Elizabeth, so what could Elizabeth do?

Elizabeth kept Mary in prison for a few years while she made up her mind. (It was 16 years in all Elizabeth could sometimes take a long time to make up her mind!) Then, in 1587, Mary was proved to be plotting against Elizabeth. The English Queen had to act quickly. If you were Elizabeth I what would you do? You could…

1 help poor Mary to get her Scottish throne back: after all she is related to you through Henry VII – but this would upset the Scottish Protestants and may cause a war with Scotland if the plan failed.

2 let her go abroad to Catholic France or Spain – but Mary might get those countries to join her in a war to take the English throne. The English Catholics would certainly support her.

3 hand Mary back to the Scots for trial and possible execution – but Mary is a relative.

4 execute her – but English Catholics might rebel with help from Spain and France. And could you be so cruel as to do this to a woman who came to you for help?

5 sign an order for Mary to be executed. Wait for the execution to be carried out, then try to cancel the order. When the cancellation arrives too late say, "Oh, dear! I did sign the execution order – but I never really meant it to be

delivered! It's the messenger's fault! Put him in the Tower of London!" But nobody would swallow that, and Spain or France may still attack.

6 keep Mary in prison – but English, French or Spanish Catholics may try to free her.

What did Elizabeth decide? Number 5.

The Queen's mind was greatly troubled. She signed a death warrant for Mary and gave it to Davison, her secretary. The next day she changed her mind but it was too late. The warrant was delivered and Mary was executed. William Davison was fined heavily and put in the Tower of London.

According to one account, Mary was beheaded by a clumsy executioner who took at least three blows of the axe and a bit of sawing to finish the job. This eyewitness described it...

The executioners desired her to forgive them for her death. She answered, "I forgive you with all my heart for now, I hope, you shall make an end to all my troubles."

Kneeling down upon a cushion, without any fear of death, she spoke a psalm. Then she laid down her head, putting her chin on the block. Lying very still on the block she suffered two strokes with the axe, making very little noise or none at all. And so the executioner cut off her head, sawing one little gristle. He then lifted up her head to the view of all the assembly and cried, "God save the Queen!"

Elizabeth did apologise to Mary's son, James...

My dearest brother, I want you to know the huge grief I feel for something which I did not want to happen and that I am innocent in the matter.

So that was all right!

But the Spanish didn't believe in Elizabeth's innocence – they didn't want to. King Philip II of Spain was sick of English ships raiding his own, laden with treasure from his overseas territories. Philip was a Catholic, like Mary. So he used her execution as an excuse to send a huge invasion fleet, The Armada, to take revenge for these English crimes. But that's another story...

Mary's Secret Message

Did Mary Queen of Scots deserve to die? Elizabeth had sheltered her when she fled from Scotland. How did she repay Elizabeth? By plotting with Elizabeth's enemies, especially English Catholics, to kill her. Of course Mary didn't go shouting it from the rooftops. It was a secret plot between her and the English conspirators. The leader of these treacherous plotters was a rich young Derbyshire man called Anthony Babbington.

So, if it was secret, how did Elizabeth find out about it? She found out because she had a very clever spy in her service, Sir Francis Walsingham. First, Walsingham sent servants to Mary's prison who pretended to work for Mary ... in fact they were spying on her.

Every time Mary sent a letter to Babbington the servants took it to Walsingham first. Mary tried writing in code. But she had sent the code to Babbington first. Walsingham had a copy. This is Mary's code…

A	B	C	D	E	F	G	H	I	J	K	L	M
○	‡	∧	⧺	ɑ	□	⊕	∞	ı		δ	∩	ɕ

N	O	P	Q	R	S	T	U	V	W	X	Y	Z
⊘	▽	s	m	⨍	Ɛ	⊿	C	V	w	7	8	9

OF	THE	NOT	FROM	YOU
▭	ꝑ	×	⨯⨯	⫯

And this is part of the message that Walsingham read and passed on to Queen Elizabeth – the part that led to Mary's execution. Use the code to read it.

LET THE GREAT PLOT GO AHEAD
SIGNED
MARY

You could try writing your own messages in this code.

Elizabeth I's sharp and cruel tongue

It was said that if someone tall disagreed with her she would promise…

I will make you shorter by a head.

She seemed to have a thing about height. She asked a Scot how tall Mary Queen of Scots was. The man replied that Mary was taller than Elizabeth. Elizabeth said… *She is too tall, then; for I myself am neither too tall nor too short.* And, of course, Elizabeth then went on to make Mary Queen of Scots "shorter by a head"!

Elizabeth also made her favourite the Earl of Essex "shorter by a head" when he tried to lead a rebellion against her in February 1601. She was so fond of him that she wore his ring for the rest of her life. It must have upset her to order his execution … though not as much as it upset Essex.

Elizabeth's "wedding" ring

Elizabeth was the last Tudor because she never married and had children. Some people dared to hint that she should marry. Her reply was:

I have already joined myself in marriage to a husband, namely the kingdom of England.

Then she would show her coronation ring. She went on:

Do not blame me for the miserable lack of children; for every one of you are children of mine.

But, when Elizabeth grew old and fat, the ring began to cut into her finger. She had to have it sawn off in January 1603. The superstitious Tudors saw this as a sign that her "marriage" to the country was ended. Two months later she was dead.

Not a lot of people know that...

...Elizabeth was one of the cleanest women in England. She was proud of the fact that she took a bath once every three months. One person was amazed and reported that she had four baths a year *whether she needed it or not*! (Even 100 years later King Louis XIV of France only had three baths in his whole life!)

...Elizabeth was' a fan of an early sort of five-a-side tennis...

About three o'clock, ten men hung up lines in a square grass court in front of her majesty's windows.

They squared out the form of the court making a cross line in the middle. Then in this square (having taken off their doublets) they played five on each side, with a small ball, to the great liking of her highness...

Queen Elizabeth owned the first wristwatch in the world. Perhaps she lost it, because her dying words were...

All my possessions for a moment of time.

Terrible Tudor joke...

The Tudors were Henry VII, Henry VIII, Edward VI and Mary ... but who came after Mary?

Answer: Her little lamb.

Terrible Tudor witches

Black cats and broomsticks

Witches casting magic spells then flying off on their broomsticks. They make great stories. But few people believe them today. The Tudors, though, thought that witches were capable of anything. And unfortunately for the so-called witches, the Tudors believed the best way to deal with a witch was to burn him or her. (Seven out of every ten people accused of being witches were women.) Some "witches" believed they would be spared if they admitted they were witches. In 1565 Elizabeth Francis confessed…

I learnt this art of witchcraft at the age of twelve years from my grandmother. She told me to renounce God and his word and to give my blood to Satan. She gave me Satan in the form of a white spotted cat. She taught me to feed the cat with bread and milk and to call it by the name of Satan.

When I first had the cat Satan I asked it to make me rich. He promised me I should and asked what I would like (for the cat spoke to me in a strange, hollow voice). I said, "Sheep," and this cat at once brought 18 sheep to my pasture, black and white. They stayed with me for a time, but in the end did all vanish away. I know not how.

I then asked for a husband, this Francis whom I now have, and the cat promised that I should have him. We were married and had a child but we did not live as quietly as I'd hoped. So I willed Satan to kill my six-month old child and he did.

When I still could not find a quiet life I asked it to make my husband lame. It did it in this way. It came one morning to Francis' shoe, lying in it like a toad. As he put on the shoe he touched it with his foot and he was taken with a lameness that will not heal.

Elizabeth said that she gave the cat to her friend Agnes Waterhouse. Agnes claimed that the cat...

killed a pig
killed three of a priest's pigs
drowned a cow
drowned geese
killed a neighbour
killed her husband.

Elizabeth Francis went to prison for a year - by confessing to her witchcraft she saved her life. Agnes Waterhouse was hanged.

The truth about Margaret

If you were Margaret Harkett's judge you might decide...

1 William Goodwin hated the old woman because she was a beggar and a nuisance.

2 Goodwin's lamb must have been sick because healthy lambs aren't brought into the kitchen.

3 The lamb dying at the same time as Margaret's visit was just bad luck – coincidence.

You might also decide...

1 Mrs Frynde was upset and bitter at the death of her husband and wanted to blame someone.

2 Frynde's fall from the pear tree was bad luck.

3 It was odd that Frynde never mentioned the curse until he was dying.

4 Frynde died of one of the many illnesses of those times or as a result of the fall.

Do you judge Margaret Harkett "Guilty" or "Not Guilty"? What did her judge do in 1585?

Margaret was executed. So were hundreds of other old women who were simply blamed for any accidents or illnesses in the area. They were usually alone – they had no one to stand up for them. They were usually too weak to stand up to their bullying neighbours.

Which is witch?

The Tudors had a way of testing a person for witchcraft. They would put the suspected witch into a sack and throw them into a nearby pond or stream. If s/he floated then s/he was a witch and would be taken out and executed. If s/he sank then s/he was innocent ... but probably dead from drowning.

Another test was to have the accused witch recite the *Lord's Prayer* without one mistake – could you do that, knowing that the first slip and you would die?

Witch fact...

In the sixteenth and seventeenth centuries about 100,000 people in Europe were accused of being witches and were killed.

Witchcraft laws

Witchcraft wasn't seen as particularly serious until 1542, when it became punishable by death if it was used for...

...discovering treasure

...injuring others

...unlawful love

In 1569 a list of magical practices that were banned included...

...curing men or beasts

...summoning wicked spirits

...telling where things were lost

Tudor superstitions

The death rate from disease was very high in Tudor times. Babies were especially likely to die from an illness. With so much death around the Tudors tried their own type of "witchcraft" to keep death and bad luck away. They didn't call their actions "witchcraft" - they called it "superstition". Some of the things they believed may seem odd to us today. They believed...

...when a baby was born they must ring church bells to frighten away evil spirits. Sometimes evil fairies stole the child and left a wicked fairy child in its place (a changeling).

…it was unlucky to wrap a new-born baby in new clothes, so it spent the first few hours of its life wrapped in an old cloth or in the clothes of older brothers or sisters. The baby had to be carried upstairs before it was carried downstairs.

…the twelfth night after Christmas was another time when evil spirits were flying around – protect yourself by chalking a cross on the beams of your house.

…it was unlucky if a hare ran in front of you – **hares**, they thought, were one of the shapes that a witch took to get around the country quickly! (Witches also disguised themselves as cats, dogs, rats, toads, wasps or butterflies. They would be fed with milk, bread and blood sucked from the witch.)

THAT'S NO REGULAR BUTTERFLY !!

…it was unlucky to leave empty eggshells lying about – they could become a witch's boat.

…in an ancient way to tell your fortune. You had to jump over a lighted candle. If the candle stayed lit then good luck was coming … but if the candle went out then bad luck was sure to follow. Which nursery rhyme describes this fortune-telling method?

Answer: Jack be nimble, Jack be quick,
Jack jump over the candlestick

Witch ghosts

In Buxted, Sussex, there is a lane called Nan Tuck's Lane. Nan Tuck had been accused of being a witch and the villagers tried to drown her. Nan escaped but was later found hanging in a nearby wood. Her ghost can be still seen running to the safety of the church, along Nan Tuck's Lane.

It is said that the screams of witches tortured by the witch-finder general can be heard in the dead of night at Seafield Bay in Suffolk.

Anne Chattox, the head of a group of Lancashire witches, was accused of digging up three skulls from a churchyard to use in a spell. She was hanged.

Father Ambrose Barlow's skull can be seen not far away, at Wardley Hall in Lancashire. He was a Catholic priest who died for his faith. The legend goes that this skull must not be disturbed in any way ... or else it will give the most blood-chilling scream you ever heard!

Terrible Tudor food

Foul facts on food

Tudor women, men and children in England drank beer, wine, sherry (or "sack"), mead and cider. This was not because they were drunkards. It was because the water was not fit to drink unless boiled.

The rich could buy or hunt for a wide range of meats. The poor had very little meat. Their main food was bread. Sometimes they caught rabbits, hares or fish to go with their turnips, beans and cabbage.

Tudor people were keen on spices. Most of the food was heavily salted to stop it going bad, so spices helped to disguise the salty taste. It also disguised the taste of rotten meat! Cinnamon, cloves, garlic and vinegar were all used.

Sugar was a rare luxury but, when they could get some, they used it on most of their food ... including meat! Their other means of sweetening food was with honey.

Hot cross buns were made at Easter- but not always eaten - they were kept as luck charms instead!

Sailors had too much salt meat and not enough fresh vegetables on their long sea journeys. As a result they developed a disease called scurvy. Their gums began to rot, their breath to smell and their teeth began to drop out. Henry VIII's ship, the *Mary Rose*, was sunk in 1545 but recovered in 1982. The sailors had drowned, but modern-day tests show that many were already dying of scurvy.

People who went to see a play would usually eat while they watched. The actors could be really put off by people cracking nuts or trampling on the shells while they tried to act!

Four-and-twenty blackbirds baked in a pie? Not so daft a rhyme. Tudors and Stuarts loved eating birds – favourites were peacocks, larks and seagulls. And not just dead birds. This incredible recipe was included in a cookery book…

TO MAKE PIES THAT THE BIRDS MAY BE ALIVE IN THEM AND FLY OUT WHEN IT IS CUT UP

∞

Make the piecrust of a great pie.
Fill it full of flour and bake it.
Being baked, open a hole at the bottom
and take out the flour.
Then having a real pie the size of the hole,
put it inside the piecrust. Put under the
piecrust, around the real pie, as many
small live birds as the empty piecrust will
hold.
This to be done before such a time as you
send the pie to the table and set it before
the guests
Uncovering, or cutting up the great lid of
the pie, all the birds will fly out, which is
a delight and a pleasure to the guests.
So that they may not be hungry, you shall
cut open the small pie.   ye woman's weekly pg 76

Got that? A big, **fake** piecrust covers a small, **real** pie **and** a flock of birds, yes? But the recipe doesn't explain what the birds are doing to the small pie - or what they are doing on the small pie - while they are waiting to be released.

Tudor foods you may want to eat

EGGS IN MUSTARD SAUCE

Ingredients:
Eggs- one for each person
& for each egg -
25 g butter
5 ml mustard (1 teaspoon)
5 ml vinegar (1 teaspoon)
A pinch of salt

Cooking:
Boil the eggs for 5 to 6 minutes.
While the eggs are boiling put the butter in a small saucepan and heat it.
When the butter has melted and begins to turn brown, take it off the heat.
Stir in the salt, mustard and vinegar.
When the eggs are ready remove the shells, cut them into quarters and put them on a warm dish.
Heat up the sauce again and pour it over the eggs.

ye woman's weekly pg 77

JUMBLES (KNOTTED BISCUITS)

Ingredients:

2 eggs   15 ml aniseed or caraway (3 teasp)

100 sugar   175 g plain flour

Cooking:

Beat the eggs. Add the sugar and aniseed (or caraway) and beat again. Stir in the flour to make a thick dough. Knead the dough on a floured board. Make the dough into rolls 1cm wide by 10 cm long. Tie the strips into a single knot. Drop the knotted dough (6 at a time) into a pan of boiling water. They will sink to the bottom so use a spoon after a minute to help them float to the top. When the knots have floated for a minute and swelled, take them out of the water and let them drain on a wire rack. Put the knots on buttered baking sheets and bake for 15 minutes at Gas Mark 4 (or 350 degrees F. or 180 degrees C.). Turn them over and bake for another 10 minutes until they are golden brown.

A Tudor guide to table manners

Do you ever get nagged for your behaviour at the dinner table? So did Tudor children. These complaints may sound familiar. A 1577 Tudor book suggested...

At the table you must...
not make faces
Scratch not thy head with thy fingers when thou art at meat.
not shout
Fill not thy mouth too full, lest thou perhaps must speak.
not gulp down drink too fast
Pick not thy teeth with thy knife nor with thy finger end.
not shuffle feet not blow on food to cool it
Nor blow out thy crumbs when thou dost eat.
not take all the best food for yourself
Foul not the place with spitting where thou dost sit.

Terrible Tudor greed

The rich would eat much more than the poor. One feast for Henry VIII at Greenwich Palace lasted seven hours. Breakfast for the poor would be boringly the same every day – bread and ale; sometimes porridge made with peas or beans.

The tables of the rich would be laid with the usual salt, bread, napkins, spoons and cups. But each guest used his or her own knife.

And where were the plates? They used large slabs of bread called "trenchers" instead. The food was served straight onto that.

Every type of fish, meat and pastry was eaten, along with 20 types of jelly. The jellies were made into the shapes of castles and animals of various descriptions.

In November 1531, Henry had five banquets at which he and his guests ate...

24 beefs
100 fat muttons
51 great veals
34 porks
91 pigs
over 700 cocks and hens
444 pigeons
168 swans
over 4000 larks.

YOU SHOULD HAVE SEEN YESTERDAY'S BREAKFAST

Many dishes were more for show than eating. A peacock would be skinned, roasted, then put back into its skin for serving. A "cockatrice" would be made by sewing the front half of a cockerel onto the back half of a baby pig before roasting.

Terrible Tudor fun and games

Blood sports

In the Middle Ages people worked long hours, but they had as much as one day in three as a holy day (a saint's day usually) or holiday. What did they do?

And what did they do on those long dark winter nights? No television or radio or records or cinema. They played sports, played games and watched sports. Some are quite similar to today's. Others are very, very different!

Animal torture

In Southwark, London, there are two bear gardens with bears, bulls and other beasts to be baited in a plot of ground for the beholders to stand safe.

A 1599 report described this "sport"...
Every Sunday and Wednesday in London there are bear baitings. The bear pit is circular with stands around the top for spectators. The ground space down below is empty.

Here a large bear on a rope was tied to a stake. Then a number of great English Mastiff dogs were brought in and shown to the bear.

After this they baited the bear, one after the other. Although the dogs were struck and mauled by the bear they did not give in. They had to be pulled off by sheer force and their mouths forced open with long sticks. The bear's teeth were not sharp and they could not injure the dogs; they have them broken short.

When the first mastiffs tired, fresh ones were brought in to bait the bear. When the bear was tired a powerful white bull was then brought in. One dog at a time was set on him. He speared these with his horns and tossed them so they could not get the better of him. And, as the dogs fell to the floor again, several men held sticks under them to break their fall. Lastly they brought in an old, blind bear which boys hit with canes and sticks. But he knew how to untie his lead, and he ran back to his stall.

The audience might bet on which one would win.

In Congleton, Cheshire, the town had its own bear. The bear died in 1601. There is a story that the Corporation wanted a new one but didn't have the money ... so they ordered the town bible to be sold to pay for it!

Football

Rules:

The pitch - could be the land between one village and the next - even if it is several miles. The ball - a pig's bladder or a ball of rags. Scoring - the team that gets the ball back to their village is the winner. Referee - none. Playing rules - none. Get the ball any way you can.

Match Commentary...

Doesn't every player in a football game lie in wait for his opponent, seeking to knock him down or punch him on the nose? Sometimes the players' necks are broken, sometimes their backs, sometimes their arms and legs are thrust out of joint, and sometimes their noses gush with blood.

Hunting for fish

The rich used to hunt for small animals using trained hawks. But there was also a sport of using birds to hunt for fish. First a cormorant, a diving sea bird, was trained to come back to its owner. When it was trained its head was covered with a mask and it was taken to the sea. At the sea shore it was unmasked and allowed to fly over the sea with a leather band around its neck. When it caught a fish it would return to the owner ... but the poor bird couldn't swallow the fish because the leather band was fastened too tight. The owner simply took the fish from the poor cormorant's beak!

Public executions

Very popular. The person to be executed would always dress in their finest clothes and make a speech so the spectators felt they had been to a good "show".

Play it yourself

Stoolball (Tudor Cricket)

1 Pitch two posts about four metres apart.
2 Use a bundle of rags for a ball.
3 Use a stick as a bat.

The bowler tries to stand at one post and hit the other post with the ball, while the batter tries to hit the ball. If the bowler hits the post then the batter is "out" and the next member of the team has a turn. If the batter hits the ball to a fielder he can be caught out.

The batter scores by hitting the ball and running from post to post and back again. The team that scores the most runs is the winner.

Loggats

Plant a stick in the ground, a "stake". Each player takes turns in throwing smaller sticks, "loggats". The player whose "loggat" finishes nearest the "stake" is the winner. You can invent your own scoring system.

Tame games

Table games

Dice, cards, dominoes, backgammon, chess and draughts were popular in Tudor times as they are today.

Here are some Tudor games you can try for yourself…

Hazard

You need two dice and any number of players.
1 Everyone throws two dice. The highest scorer is the "Caster".
2 The Caster throws until s/he gets 5, 6, 7, 8 or 9. The number s/he gets is the "Main Point".
3 The Caster throws again until s/he gets a number 4, 5, 6, 7, 8, 9 or 10. This is the "Chance Point". The "Chance Point" cannot be the same as the "Main Point".

4 The Caster throws again and tries to get the Chance Point – if s/he does then s/he is the winner.

5 If the Caster throws the "Main Point" before s/he manages to throw another "Chance Point" then s/he loses.

6 Use matchsticks to gamble with. If the Caster wins, s/he takes one matchstick from each player. If the Caster loses then s/he pays out a matchstick to each other player.

7 Once the Caster loses s/he passes the dice to the next player who throws for a new "Main Point" and a new "Chance Point".

Trump

You need a pack of playing cards and two or more players.

1 Place a pack of cards on the table face down.

2 Turn one card over. That number card is the "Trump".

3 Each person, one at a time, will turn the other cards over.

4 Every time one matches the "Trump", all the players hit the table with the left hand and shout "Trump!" Whoever is the last to shout and hit the table is out.

Merelles

You need a board marked like the one on page 101. Draw it onto a large piece of card.

You need ten counters, or coins, and two players.

1 Each player takes turns to place a counter on a dot.

2 The aim is to place three counters in a row.

3 If all the counters are on the board and there are no rows of three then the players can begin to move their counters.

4 A player can only move to an open dot and only one space each turn.

5 The first to get a row of three is the winner.

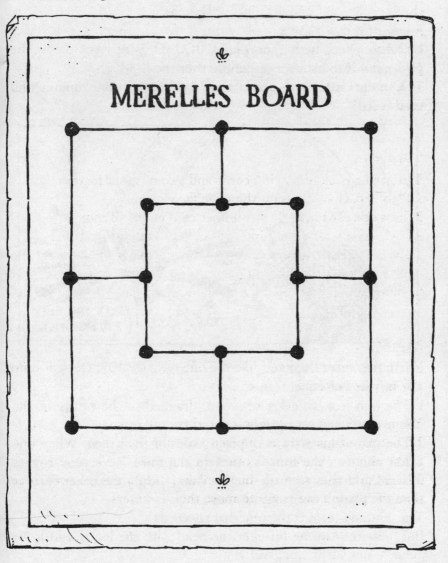

MERELLES BOARD

Some Tudor games you shouldn't play

Cudgelling

A game for two players.
1 Each is armed with a short stick.
2 The aim is to hit your opponent over the head.
3 A point is scored every time you make your opponent's head bleed!

NEXT TIME I GET THE BIG STICK!

Dun the cart-horse

A game for two equal teams.
1 The dun is a large log of wood, dragged to the centre of the village green and set upright.
2 The two teams start at opposite sides of the green. When one player shouts, "the dun is stuck in the mire," everyone rushes forward and tries to push the log over – while the other team is trying to push it over towards you.
The winning team is the one that succeeds.
But, beware! Anyone hit over the head with the log is said to be "Out" – not surprising, really!

Hurling

A game for two teams of 15 to 30 players.

1 A wooden ball is boiled in candle-grease to make it more slippery.

2 The aim is to pick up the ball and run through the other team's "goal".

3 If a player with the ball is tackled, he must pass the ball but he can only pass it backwards.

4 If your team don't have the ball then your aim is to stop the other team scoring – stop them any way you can!

Tudor sports reports

The Prior of Bicester Abbey has been paying money to players who play football on holidays. They are England's first professional footballers.

1491. Golf has been banned in Scotland by law because it's a wasteful pastime.
In no place in the country shall there be football, golf or other such unprofitable sports.

1513. King Henry VIII is so keen on bowling at Skittles that he took a portable bowling alley with him on a trip to France.

Terrible Tudor sailors

The sailors of Tudor Times are legendary for their daring exploits – trips around the earth in little leaking boats, fighting the mighty Spanish, French and Dutch navies, roaming the oceans with piratical plots.

Sir Francis Drake was the scourge of the oceans. He raided the coasts of the Caribbean and South America, sucking the wealth from these Spanish territories. As Drake filled Queen Elizabeth's coffers with plundered gold, she gave him more and more little jobs to do, such as helping to defeat the great Spanish Armada in 1588. It is of no surprise that many legends have been woven round Drake's cunning exploits. And wherever there are legends there are lies. Could you sort out the historical from the hysterical?

Hearing and believing

Drake's Drum

From 1577 till 1580 Sir Francis Drake sailed around the world in the service of Elizabeth I. At last, in the West Indies in 1596, he lay dying. He sent for his drum, an instrument that his men believed had magical powers. He ordered that it be sent back to England. He swore that he would return to defend his homeland if anyone beat the drum when England was in danger.

The drum was taken back to Buckland Abbey near Plymouth, where it remains to this day. The legend has changed a little over the years. The drum beats out its own warning when the country is in danger.

The drum is said to have rattled when Napoleon Bonaparte was brought to Plymouth after the battle of Waterloo. It seemed to know that the great enemy of England was nearby.

Then it has been heard three times this century. It sounded in 1914 when the first World War started; it sounded towards the end of that war when it had been taken on board the Royal Navy flagship, *The Royal Oak*.

When it sounded on *The Royal Oak*, the German fleet were approaching. They were heading towards the British fleet in order to surrender ... perhaps it was giving a "Victory" salute.

Men were sent twice to find out where the noise of the drum was coming from - and twice they returned with no answer. The commander searched the ship for himself ... and found nothing. Every sailor was at battle-stations in the ship. No one could have played the drum. *The Royal Oak* dropped anchor.

The drum-roll stopped as mysteriously as it had started.

The last time the drum was heard was in the darkest hours of World War Two. The British forces had crossed the channel to attack Hitler's German army. They were being driven back to the beaches. The German army was closing in, ready to massacre them. A miracle was needed.

The drum was heard sounding – the miracle occurred! A fleet of little British boats set off from the fishing ports and coastal towns of Eastern England. Somehow they crossed the channel, rescued huge numbers of men, then brought them safely home.

Was Sir Francis Drake watching over this feat of sea bravery, which was surely as great as his own trip round the world?

The Spanish Armada – Who won? Who lost?

The Spanish Armada, its special date
Is fifteen hundred and eighty-eight.

King Philip II of Spain was fed up with the English. His wife had been Mary I, Queen of England. He reckoned that he should be king, now that she was dead. But Elizabeth had grabbed the throne.
Also, English sailors were roaming the high seas and attacking the Spanish ships and colonies for their riches.

 Why was the Spanish Armada so expensive to run?

Because they only got 20 miles to the galleon.

Worse, Philip was Catholic and Elizabeth I was a Protestant, chopping off Catholic heads. In 1587 she had Mary Queen of Scots executed. This was the last straw as far as Philip was concerned.

So, in 1588 he decided it was time to teach the English a lesson once and for all. He assembled a huge fleet, an "Armada" of 130 galleons, and sent his armies off to invade England. They failed. This is what happened…

5 THE SPANISH FLEET SAILED UP THE ENGLISH CHANNEL

KEEP TOGETHER LADS, STRAIGHT LINE AT THE SPEED OF THE SLOWEST VESSEL

THEY WERE SITTING DUCKS FOR THE SMALLER FASTER ENGLISH SHIPS

6

SITTING DUCKS - OR DO I MEAN SITTING DRAKES

7 BUT THE ENGLISH DIDN'T DARE GET TOO CLOSE TO THE HUGE SPANISH GUNS

HA! YOU SANK JUST TWO SHIPS! WATER OFF A SITTING-DUCKS BACK!

8 THE SPANISH REACHED CALAIS FAIRLY SAFELY...

CALAIS

NOW I'VE GOT THEM! REMEMBER CADIZ?

9 THE ENGLISH ATTACKED THE SPANISH SHIPS WITH FIREBOATS. THEY WERE TRAPPED IN THE HARBOUR

CURSES! WHAT SHALL WE DO?

PANIC, CAPTAIN!

10 THE SPANISH PANICKED AND BLUNDERED ABOUT

ANOTHER 14 GONE ONLY 114 TO GO!

11 THEN THE SPANISH HAD SOME REALLY BAD LUCK! A STORM DROVE THEM OUT INTO THE NORTH SEA AND WRECKED THEM

THE PROTESTANT WIND HAS WRECKED 50 MORE SHIPS

AND IT'S MADE ME AS SEA-SICK AS A PARROT!

12 THE ENGLISH HAD SUNK 16 SPANISH SHIPS – THE STORM HAD SUNK 60 THAT'S WHY THE ARMADA MEDAL THAT WAS AWARDED TO THE ENGLISH SAILORS SAID :

GOD BREATHED AND THEY WERE SCATTERED

Of 130 galleons that left Spain in the summer of 1588, only about 50 returned in late September. As many as 19,000 Spaniards are thought to have died – it took them so long to sail back to Spain that many who didn't drown starved instead.

But the English sailors had their problems, too. In August 1588 the English Admiral, Lord Howard, wrote...

The sailors cry out for money and know not when they are to be paid. I have given them my word and honour that I will see them paid. If I had not done so they would have run away from Plymouth in their thousands.

But worse was to follow. Just the next day, Howard was writing...

Sickness and death begin to wonderfully grow among us. It is a most pitiful sight to see, here at Margate, how the men, having no place to go, die in the streets. It would grieve any man's heart to see them that have served so bravely to die so miserably.

So, Elizabeth won – she kept her throne. But who really lost? The English sailors? The Spanish sailors? Or both?

Sir Walter Raleigh

Sir Walter Raleigh was a sailor, too ... **and** a writer, **and** explorer. He was a favourite of Queen Elizabeth I. A lot of stories have been told about him ... but are they all true?

Try these questions on your teacher. All they have to answer is 'True" or "False".

1 Walter Raleigh once spread his cloak in the mud for Queen Elizabeth to walk over.
True or False?

2 Walter Raleigh was the first man to bring potatoes to England. *True or False?*

3 Walter Raleigh was the first man to bring tobacco to England. *True or False?*

Answer: All are False!

110

The Truth About Walter

1 Most people have heard the story of Sir Walter Raleigh and the cloak. It was supposed to have happened when Raleigh was a young man. The queen was passing through crowds of her people when she reached a muddy puddle in the road. She stopped. After all, she didn't want to spoil her fine shoes.

Quick-thinking Walter Raleigh pulled off his new cloak and covered the puddle so she could step over without walking through mud. The queen smiled. Walter's act was to make him a rich and powerful favourite of the queen.

A great story. But a true story? No. It originated with Thomas Fuller who was a historian of the 17th century who liked to "dress up" boring history with lively little incidents like the story of Raleigh's cloak ... even if they didn't really happen!

2 Walter Raleigh's potatoes? For hundreds of years Walter Raleigh teachers have taught that Raleigh brought the first potatoes to England when he returned from a voyage to America in 1586. But there is no evidence from Tudor times to say this happened. A book called *Herball* (written by John Gerard in 1597) talks about someone called Clusius who had grown potatoes in Italy in 1585. The vegetable became very popular and was grown everywhere in Europe within ten years.

3 Walter Raleigh's tobacco? Again there are records of tobacco being used in France in 1560 - 26 years before Raleigh's ships returned from Virginia. It was brought there by John Nicot (whose name gives us "Nicotine"). It must have crossed the English Channel long before Raleigh's ships even set off.

In 1573 William Harrison wrote ...

In these days the taking in of the Indian herb called "Tobacco" is greatly taken up in England. It is used against rheums and other diseases of the lungs with great effect.

But not everyone agreed. In 1614, Barnaby Rich was writing...
They say tobacco is good for a cold, rheums, for aches, for dropsies and for all manner of diseases. But I see the ones who smoke most are as affected by those diseases as much as the ones who don't. It is now sold in every tauern, inn and ale-house as much as beer.

Oddly enough, the man who hated tobacco smoking the most was King James I. He wrote that smoking was...
A custom loathsome to the eye, hateful to the nose, harmful to the brain and dangerous to the lungs.

(If Raleigh really **did** smoke and James I was the first anti-smoking campaigner, then James was a great success. In 1618 he cured Raleigh's "loathsome" habit for good. James had Raleigh's head cut off for treason!)

112

What is it?

Drake found some new foods on his journey round the world. But what were they?

1 *We found a plant with a fruit as big as a man's head. Having taken off the back (which is full of string) you shall come to a hard shell which holds a pint of sweet liquid. Within that shell you will find a white, hard substance as sweet as almonds and half an inch thick.*

2 *We found a store of great fowl which could not fly, the bigness of geese, whereof we killed 3000 in less than one day.*

Terrible Tudor clothes

Did you know?

It was during the Tudor period that English clothes for the rich became exciting and different. Merchants were in touch with countries as far away as Russia and America. While the Tudor poor still wore rough woollen clothes, the Tudor rich were better dressed than ever before with velvets and satins from Italy, lace from France and starch from Holland. And starch meant they could make those stiff collars, "Ruffs", that were so popular in Elizabeth's time. But...

Ten things you probably didn't know...

1 Sometimes the stiff ruffs were so wide that ladies couldn't reach their mouths to eat! Silversmiths had to make extra-long spoons for them.

2 Ruffs were usually white but could be another colour. Yellow ruffs were popular for a while. Then a famous murderess, Mrs Turner, was hanged wearing one. They suddenly went out of fashion!

3 A puritan, Philip Stubbes, claimed...

The devil invented these great ruffs. But if it happen that a shower of rain catch them, then their great ruffs fall, as dishcloths fluttering in the wind.

4 Henry VIII looks very fat in his portraits. But as well as having an over-fed body, his clothes were thick with padding- at least it kept him warm in his draughty castles.

5 The Elizabethan ladies' fashion was for tiny waists. To help them squeeze into smart dresses, the ladies (and even the girls) wore iron corsets.

6 Girls showed that they were unmarried by wearing no hat in public.

7 Elizabethan men wore short trousers called "hose". They had to pad them so they wouldn't show any creases. They weren't too fussy what they padded them with - horsehair (itchy!), rags or even bran (horsefood)! If the "hose" split the bran would run.

8 Poor country girls often wore shoes with iron rings under them. Sometimes they had thick wooden soles. This was to keep their skirts out of the deep mud and rubbish in the streets and market places.

 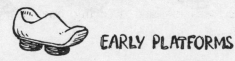

EARLY PLATFORMS

9 In 1571, Elizabeth's parliament made a law forcing all married women to wear white knitted caps, and all men (over the age of six) to wear woollen hats. The caps and hats had to be knitted in England using English wool. Elizabeth got a lot of taxes from the wool trade – English wool was in great demand from other countries, too.

10 Aprons were quite a new idea in Tudor times. You could often tell a man's occupation from the design of his apron...

millers and cooks	– white
barbers	– checked
builders and blacksmiths	– leather

I'M GLAD I DON'T HAVE TO WEAR THAT

Terrible Tudor trousers

If you'd like to act like a Tudor, feel like a Tudor, or if you're off to a fancy dress party, you may like to try making these Tudor "hose".

1 Wear a pair of tights or tight trousers first.

2 Take a pair of old, baggy trousers. Cut them off at the knee. Slit them as shown.

3 Put the baggy trousers on over the tights. Tie them at the knee with ribbon or a scarf.

4 Stuff the baggy trousers with material of a different colour so it shows through the slits.

5 Wear a loose shirt and ruff and a belt with a sword or dagger - wooden, of course.

6 Go around saying, *To be* or *not to be*, or *Alas, poor Yorick*. (They're famous lines from William Shakespeare plays - adults and teachers will be totally impressed.)

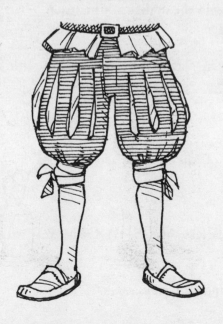

A ruff idea

1 Take seven 24 cm doilies (lacey paper table decorations, usually used at parties).

2 Cut them in half.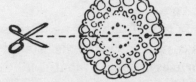

Use sticky tape to attach them to a 4 m strip of ribbon, allowing enough ribbon to tie at the back.

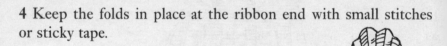

3 Make 2 cm folds in the doilies folding each one into a fan shape.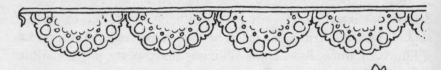

4 Keep the folds in place at the ribbon end with small stitches or sticky tape.

5 Tie the ends of the ribbon around your neck.

6 Wear with a collarless shirt (boys). Girls, wear with a blouse and full-length skirt.

7 Stroll around singing *Greensleeves*.

Terrible Tudor life for women

A woman's life is hard in ten terrible ways...

1 Girls could marry at 12 (boys at 14). This was usually arranged by their parents. They would still live with their parents at this age, though.

2 Many upper-class girls were married by 15. At the age of 16 they could live with their husbands.

3 It wasn't usually considered worth the money to send a girl to school. Her mother could teach her all the household crafts she would need to be a useful wife.

4 If a girl didn't marry there wasn't much she could do. The convents had been abolished by Henry VIII so she couldn't become a nun. Very often, unmarried girls would have to stay at home with their parents and spin. That's why they became known as "spinsters" - a word we still use.

JUST BECAUSE I DIDN'T GET MARRIED WHEN I WAS STILL PLAYING WITH MY TEDDY MEANS I'VE GOT TO SIT AND SPIN FOR THE REST OF MY LIFE

5 One farmer described a good wife's behaviour. He said she should...

pray when first getting out of bed, then clean the house, lay the table, milk the cows, dress her children, cook meals for the household, brew and bake when needed, send corn to the mill, make butter and cheese, look after the swine and collect the eggs.

6 Anthony Fitzherbert added to that list and said she should...

shear corn and in time of need help her husband to fill the dung cart, drive the plough, load hay and go to market to sell butter, cheese, milk, eggs, chickens, pigs, geese and all manner of corn. (What did he expect her to do in her spare time?!)

7 But English women were better off than those in other countries – at least, that's what the men said! Thomas Platter said that...

the womenfolk of England have more freedom than in any other land. The men must put up with such ways and may not punish them for it. Indeed, the good wives often beat the men.

8 Girls were expected to help in the house by collecting fine feathers (down) for mattresses, making candles, spinning, weaving and embroidering. Once every three months, the household tablecloths and bed-clothes were washed; the girls were expected to help with this.

9 Women could be punished for nagging or "scolding". A court record from 1592 says...

The wife of Walter Hycocks and the wife of Peter Phillips are common scolds. Therefore it is ordered that they shall be told in church to stop their scolding. But, if their neighbours complain a second time, they shall be punished by the ducking stool.

And "the ducking stool" meant being tied to a chair and lowered into a nearby river.

I NOTICE IT'S ALWAYS THE MEN DOING THE DUCKING!

10 If the ducking stool didn't work then there was the "branks" – an iron mask that clamped onto the head with a metal bar going into the woman's mouth to hold her tongue down. Wearing the branks, a woman would be paraded round the town to show other women what might happen to them.

AAS ANANA INGOW AIR OO EH EN OO ISS ING ON EE, IH OO ING ISS IS AHING OO AI ILL I EH IH OH EN OOL EAR UNING ASS OR URE!!!

HOME SWEET HOME

Miss World – Tudor style

The Elizabethans had a clear idea of what a beautiful woman should look like. Here's a shopping list...

1 extremely white skin
2 blue eyes
3 ruby-red lips
4 fair hair

You don't fit the description? Never mind, you can always change if you want.

Dark hair can be bleached with a mixture of sulphur and lead. This will, unfortunately, make it fall out in time. Never mind, as an Elizabethan said, Elizabethan girls are...

not simply content with their own hair, but buy other hair either of horse, mare or any other strange beast,

Skin too dark? A deadly mixture of lead and vinegar can be plastered on. (This has the same effect as making an Egyptian mummy.)

Lips too pale? Lipstick could be made from egg whites and cochineal - what is "cochineal"? It's a dye made from crushed cochineal beetles.

THREE SIMPLE STEPS TO A MORE BEAUTIFUL YOU!

Eyes don't sparkle enough? Drop in some belladonna (which means, "beautiful lady"!) to make them look larger. Keep it away from your lips, though. Belladonna is a poisonous drug made from deadly-nightshade.

If a mother wanted her daughter to grow up beautiful she was advised to bathe her in milk to give her a pale skin. Unwanted freckles? (Definitely out of fashion.) Treat with "brimstone" (sulphur).

Smelly? **Don't** have a bath! (Baths aren't considered "healthy"!) Just cover up the smell with perfume.

So...

Would you like to have been a Tudor woman or girl? In fact, would you have liked to live in the Terrible Tudor times at all? The Golden Age" of Good Queen Bess and Jolly Old Henry VIII?

Every age has its problems. But, as a historian once said...

In reviewing the past I think that we of the present day have much to be thankful for.

You've reviewed some of the Tudor past in this book. So, are you "thankful" that you didn't live then? Or do you agree with the history book that said it was an extremely exciting time to be alive?

Epilogue

Old Elizabeth died and the last of the terrible Tudors was gone. Mary Queen of Scots was dead too... but her son, James VI of Scotland, was very much alive. The first of the sinister Stuarts.

The Stuart family in Scotland had a history every bit as bloody and violent as the Tudors in England.

• James I was murdered in a toilet in 1437 while he was trying to defend himself with a pair of fire tongs.

• James II was killed by an exploding cannon in the seige of Roxburgh in 1460.

• James III was murdered by his nobles in 1486.

• James IV was killed at the Battle of Flodden in 1513.

• James V died of despair shortly after his defeat at the battle of Solway Floss in 1542.

• Mary Queen of Scots, as we already know, murdered her husband then fled to England to avoid the chop. Elizabeth gave it to her instead.

• James VI became the first James of England ... and the first lucky Stuart to come from Scotland. He came south and added the English throne to his collection.

Of course, not everyone was happy with James. Not everyone wanted a king with such disgusting habits! For a start, he picked his nose!

James always wore a dagger-proof vest. Who can blame him? First, some cunning Catholics tried to blow him off the throne with the gunpowder plot. Lucky James survived again! We may forget James, but we always remember the fifth of November!

And that was just the start of a dramatic century. A century of plagues and fire and plots and rebels; a century with Englishmen fighting Englishmen and Englishmen hanging witches – the Scots preferred to burn them!

If the Tudors gave their queens a sharp pain in the neck then the Stuart people gave it to one of their kings!

The Stuart times were certainly sinister. But that's another story, and another slice of Horrible History...

TERRIBLE TUDORS

GRISLY QUIZ

**Now find out if you're a
terrible Tudor expert!**

HORRIBLE HENRY

Henry VIII was one of Britain's cruellest monarchs ever. Here's a quick quiz to test your brains. Get one wrong and your head goes on the block…

1. When wife no. 1, Catherine of Aragon, died Henry had a…?
a) ball
b) fight
c) cup of tea

2. Wife no. 2, Anne Boleyn, needed the toilet a lot during her coronation. Her ladies-in-waiting kept her potty handy…?
a) under the table
b) in a room close by
c) on the throne

3. When Anne gave birth to a daughter, Henry…?
a) sulked
b) cheered
c) fell out of his pram

4. While Anne was being beheaded, Henry was playing…?
a) tennis
b) music
c) the fool

5. Henry divorced wife no. 4, Anne of Cleves, because she was…?
a) ugly
b) stupid
c) vegetarian

6. Wife no. 5, Catherine Howard, was sentenced to death for having lovers. She begged for mercy but Heartless Henry locked the door and left her...?
a) to wail
b) in jail
c) looking pale

7. Henry had his old friend Thomas More executed and his head stuck...?
a) over London Bridge
b) under London Bridge
c) in a fridge

8. Henry had Cardinal Fisher beheaded and showed disrespect by leaving the headless body...?
a) naked for a day
b) on the main highway
c) in a window display

Ingenious insults

Can you match the words in these columns to come up with ten insults that Shakespeare put into his plays? WARNING: Do NOT call your teacher any of these names.

1.	taffeta	a)	lump
2.	scurvy	b)	ape
3.	red-tailed	c)	chuff
4.	threadbare	d)	bumble-bee
5.	mad-headed	e)	punk
6.	fat	f)	juggler
7.	false	g)	crookback
8.	bloodsucker of	h)	caterpillars
9.	scolding	i)	sleeping men
10.	deformed	j)	lord

Quick Questions - Mean Queens

1. Catholic Mary came to the throne in 1553, and the Protestants showed what they thought of her by leaving something on her bed. What? (Clue: hounding her out of the palace?)

2. Mary married Spanish Prince Philip in 1554. He hated something that came from her nose. What? (Clue: 'snot what you think)

3. Philip left Mary and went to fight in Europe. She tried to tempt him back with what? (Clue: the way to a man's heart is through his stomach, they say)

4. Mary had a lot of Protestant 'heretics' burned. Her chief helper was Reginald Pole who chose really odd 'heretics' to burn. What was odd about them? (Clue: they never felt a thing)

5. Mary sent Archbishop Cranmer to the stake in 1556. He had written an apology then changed his mind. When he saw the fire he did a strange thing. What? (Clue: he went to his death single-handed)

6. Mary died and the news was taken to half-sister Elizabeth, the new queen. They say Elizabeth was reading in the garden when the news came, but that's unlikely. Why? (Clue: remember, remember when Mary died)

7. Elizabeth had a new tax created which only men could pay. It was a tax on what? (Clue: it might grow on you)

8. Elizabeth I's godson, Sir John Harrington, disgraced himself by making rude remarks to her ladies-in-waiting. She

banished him. He went off and invented something that was so useful she forgave him. What? (Clue: flushed with success?)

9. In 1576 the explorer Martin Frobisher returned to England with a load of 'black earth'. What use did he think it would be? (Clue: he thinks the soil is rich)

10. Eloye Mestrell invented the first machine in England for making coins for the government. Yet in 1578 he was arrested and executed. What was his crime? (Clue: double your money)

11. Mary Queen of Scots had Sir John Huntly beheaded but then discovered he had to be tried properly and found guilty if she was to get his fortune. What did she do? (Clue: head on over to the courtroom)

12. Mary Queen of Scots became unpopular in Scotland, and fled to England to ask cousin Elizabeth I for protection. How did Liz protect Mary? (Clue: no one can get in to get her)

13. James Douglas of Scotland invented the 'Maiden' machine. In 1581 the Maiden killed him. What was it? (Clue: a chip off the old block)

14. Mary Queen of Scots had lots of troubles. She finally met a man and thanked him for, 'making an end to all my troubles'. What was this man's job? (Clue: not an agony aunt!)

15. When Mary Queen of Scots was beheaded in 1587 her head was supposed to have been lifted high in the air by the executioner to prove she was dead. But he dropped it. Why? (Clue: hair today, gone tomorrow)

WOULD YOU BELIEVE IT?

Queen Elizabeth I ruled from 1558 to 1603. There are lots of stories about this famous queen, but which of these tall tales are true and which false...?

1. She threatened to pass a law banning her courtiers from wearing long cloaks.
2. She died because of a rotten tooth.
3. Elizabeth was overjoyed when her sister, Mary, died.
4. She liked to read her horoscope.
5. Elizabeth ate a chessboard.
6. She had regular baths.
7. Elizabeth never even considered getting married.
8. Elizabeth had beautiful red hair.
9. She was always true to her Protestant faith.
10. She punched and kicked her secretary.

Answers

Horrible Henry
1–8. All *Answers* are (a). Anyone answering (c) should give up quizzes ... now.

Ingenious insults
1.e) 2.j) 3.d) 4.f) 5.b) 6.c) 7.h) 8.i) 9.g) 10.a)

Quick Questions – Mean Queens
1. A dead dog. The head was shaved, the ears cropped and a noose put around its neck. The message was clear: 'This is what we do to Catholics.'

2. Philip hated Mary's foul breath. It was an illness she had and not her fault. But it put him off, and he left her broken hearted.

3. His favourite meat pies. She had them sent across the English Channel to him. He ate all the pies but didn't go home for more.

4. They were dead. Reggie dug them up and burned them anyway. Funny feller.

5. He stuck his writing hand in the flames to punish it for writing the apology. (No jokes about second-hand shops, please.)

6. It was November. Not many people are daft enough to sit in the garden in an English winter.

7. Beards.

8. A flushing toilet. It took him six years to invent it but Liz loved his loo.

9. He believed it contained a fortune in gold. It didn't. He was just a clueless captain.

10. Eloye made a second, secret, machine and forged money for himself. Usually forgers had a hand chopped off but Eloye was hanged.

11. Huntly's head was sewn back on and his corpse was put on trial.

12. Elizabeth locked Mary in prison. She left her there for years before deciding to execute her.

13. The Maiden was a type of guillotine. He was executed on it.

14. He was her executioner. Actually he made a messy end to her troubles, taking three chops and a bit of sawing to get the head off.

15. Mary was wearing a wig. When he grabbed it, the head slipped out and bounced on to the floor.

Would you believe it?

1. True. She was terrified of being killed and wanted her courtiers' swords uncovered and ready.

2. False. Elizabeth is famous for having rotten teeth, but that didn't kill her. She caught a cold and never recovered.

3. True. She said, 'This is the Lord's doing and it is marvellous in our eyes.'

4. True. A mathematician (and magician!) called John Dee used to read Liz's horoscope and foretell the future for her.

5. True. Of course, it was made of marzipan.

6. True. Elizabeth did bathe regularly ... once every three months!

7. False. Liz had a few close calls when it came to marriage, including Lord Dudley and the French Duke of Anjou.

8. True and False. She did at first, but she ended up bald with a collection of 80 wigs!

9. False. While Catholic Mary Tudor was queen, Elizabeth said she was a Catholic too.

10. True. Secretary William Davison was just one of the unfortunate palace workers who suffered Liz's temper tantrums.

INTERESTING INDEX

Where will you find 'blood-sucking fleas', 'smelly breath', 'swearing' and 'sewers' in an index? In a Horrible Histories book, of course!

SLIMY
STUARTS

Introduction

History can be simply horrible. This history book is simply horribly *interesting*. It will tell you things about Stuart times that not many teachers know.

James I used the power of the rack to torture Guy Fawkes. Now you can torture your teacher with ... the power of *the question!*

You can amaze your relations with terribly true tales of dreadful deeds...

Become the most popular person in your class by learning new words. Yes, even *you* can become the *dossy* with a little practice.

You'll end up knowing a bit more about life in the slimy 17th century. The funny, the foul and the fantastic. They are all here…

Slimy Stuart timeline

1603 Elizabeth I kicks the royal bucket. Last of the Tudors. James VI of Scotland comes down to be James I of England as well. First of the Stuarts.

> *Slimy Jim, snotty Jim,*
> *Slobbered when he drank*
> *his beer;*
> *Hated witches, hated ciggies.*
> *Loved to murder little deer.*

1605 A plot to blow James all the way back to Scotland is discovered – known as the Gunpowder Plot. Guy Fawkes gets the blame.

1616 Playwright, William Shakespeare, dies on his 52nd birthday. That probably spoiled the party a bit.

1621 Puritans who can't stand James settle in America. They don't bother to ask the native American Indians, of course.

1625 James I turns up his regal toes – he snuffs it. Son Charles I gets to put bum on throne.

> *Charlie One, on the run;*
> *He'd upset the Roundhead chaps.*
> *Said that God was on his side;*
> *God not there when Charlie axed!*

143

1629 Charles upsets Parliament in a row over who's in charge, them or him. Slimy Charlie says he can rule without them. And, to prove it, he does.

1637 Charles upsets the Scots by trying to force them to use his new Prayer Book. Charles has the nerve to call Parliament again to help him. Charlie and Parli just argue.

1642 War breaks out between Charlie (with his Cavaliers) and Parli (with their Roundheads). Brother fights brother.

1647 Charlie loses war and makes friends with the Scots and with Parliament. Sadly, Parliament is now ruled by its army under General Oliver Cromwell who makes sure…

1649 Charlie gets the chop. Royal head in un-royal bucket. England ruled without a king until…

1658 Oliver Cromwell dies and his son Richard takes over until…

1660 The 'Restoration' – the monarchy returns with Charles II. Cromwell dug up, strung up and beheaded – *very* slimy.

144

Charlie two used to woo
Lots of women, what a bloke!
Merry monarch – plague then fire,
Sent the laughter up in smoke.

1665 The Great Plague – in London alone 100,000 people die ... and just as many rats.

1666 The Great Fire of London – destroys many of the filthy wooden buildings that housed the plague.

1685 King Charles II sick. Given 'Spirit of Human Skull' but dies anyway. (He apologized to his doctors for taking so long to die.) Catholic brother, James II, takes over.

King Jim, rather dim;
Made it clear he liked the Pope.
Britons told him,
'Push off, Jimmy!
Catholic Britain? Not a hope.'

1688 James thrown off throne. Even his daughter, Mary, is glad to see the back of him. She takes over with hubby, William of Orange.

Mary big, ate like pig;
Willie small like her pet cat.
Smallpox killed her; as for Willie,
His horse stumbled, he went splatt!

1702 Mary's sister, Anne, takes over the throne – she doesn't share it with hubby. When you're as fat as Anne there's no room to share a throne with a pin.

Annie, stout; feet with gout;
Food and brandy she would
gorge.
Children all dead, no more
Stuarts;
Throne passed on to German
George.

1707 England and Scotland united under one Parliament.

1714 Anne pops her clogs – just as her 17 children have before her. End of slimy Stuarts.

Slimy James I (reigned 1603-1625)

The Stuarts were a funny lot ... funny-'peculiar'. *Not* so funny-'haha' if you were one of their victims. They were wheelers and dealers, always ducking and diving to keep out of trouble. You could never be quite sure what they were up to. In fact they were rather slimy characters. The slimy Stuarts.

James the slob

James was 37 when he became king of England. He had a straggling brown beard and hair, watery blue eyes and spindly legs. A French visitor described James when he was 18 years old…

He was of middle height, more fat because of his clothes than his body. His clothes always being made large and easy, the doublets quilted to be dagger-proof. His breeches were in great pleats and full stuffed. He was naturally timid, his eyes large and always rolling after any stranger came into his presence. His beard was very thin. His tongue too large for his mouth which made him drink very badly as if eating his drink which came out into the cup from each side of his mouth. His skin was soft because he never washed his hands, only rubbed his finger ends slightly with the wet end of a napkin.

And those were just his good points! Fontenay forgot to mention James was bow-legged and picked his nose. The king used his sleeve instead of a handkerchief ... though he sometimes preferred to use a finger and thumb. Maybe Fontenay didn't notice! Among James's other bad habits were swearing and drinking too much.

A famous historian called Macaulay said James was like *two* men. One was a witty scholar who argued well – the other was a 'nervous drivelling idiot'. You decide which from something that happened when he arrived in England. James complained that the people of England were forever pestering him to make a public appearance. He refused – very rudely.

A wit? Or a twit?

Killer James
James I wasn't so sure of English customs when he arrived from Scotland. On his way to be crowned in London he stopped at the town of Newark. As the crowds packed the streets to greet him a pickpocket was caught. James ordered that the pickpocket should be hanged. The obedient councillors had the man executed.

Only *then* did they quietly tell James that in England the king did not have the power to put anyone to death without trial. This was no comfort at all to the pickpocket.

On his way to London James enjoyed some hunting. To make sure the king had enough fun the English cheated. They kept hares in cages and let them out in time for the king to catch them.

Gunpowder, treason ... and lies?

Everybody knows about Guy Fawkes ... or do they? Test your teacher with these well known 'facts' about Guy Fawkes and the Gunpowder Plot. How many are true and how many false?

1 Guy Fawkes was born a Catholic.
2 Guy Fawkes was the leader of the gunpowder plot.
3 Luckily, Guy Fawkes was caught just before he blew up James and his Parliament.
4 Guy Fawkes was tortured and betrayed his friends.
5 Guy Fawkes was burned on a bonfire.

Answers: False! False! False! False! Oh, and ... false!

Here's how…

1 Guy (or Guido as he was christened) was brought up a Protestant. When he was ten his new stepfather (Denis Bainbridge) taught him to follow the Catholic religion. The Catholics had already tried to dispose of Elizabeth I (with a little help from foreign friends, Armadas and poisonous plots). James was just another Protestant monarch to be disposed of … nothing personal!

2 The leader of the Gunpowder Plot was Robert Catesby. Guy was fighting as a soldier for the Spanish army when the plot was first dreamt up. He was smuggled back into England to help – probably because he was an explosives expert.

THIS IS A BOMB

GOSH!

3 Guy was caught at least 12 hours before Parliament was due to meet the king. And it wasn't 'luck'. The soldiers who caught Guy had been tipped off and were searching for explosives when they found him there. King James had also been tipped off. He was never in any real danger from the Gunpowder Plot.

4 Guy was tortured on the rack for two days before he even gave his real name. It took another two days before he confessed to the plot then *six* more days before he named any other plotters. But, by that time, his partners had already been hunted and arrested or killed. They *had* been betrayed … but not by Guy Fawkes.

5 Guy was due to be hanged, drawn and quartered. This was the punishment for 'treason', a crime against the king. Burning was for a crime against the Church.

Slimy James

Not everybody loved James when he arrived. What James needed was to give the English a shock. He needed to say, 'You'd be worse off if I was dead!' ... then arrange an attempt on his own life. A *failed* attempt, naturally. Is that what this slimy Stuart did?

1 First find an enemy who would want James dead. The Catholics were a good choice.

2 Get spies to persuade a Catholic group to kill the king – suggest a plot to blow him up in Parliament with all his ministers.

3 Then catch them just in time.

On November 5th 1605 the king's chief minister, Robert Cecil, said...

It has pleased God to uncover a plot to kill the King, Queen, Prince and the most important men of this land, by secretly putting gunpowder into a cellar under Parliament and blowing them all up at once.

Guy Fawkes, who was caught in the cellars of the Houses of Parliament, was tortured and executed.

As an example to others, an execution for treason was super-savagely slimy. After hanging the victim for a few moments he was cut down and cut open. His guts were thrown on to a fire before he was beheaded and cut into quarters.

Guy cheated the executioner, who wanted Guy to really suffer. When the rope was placed round Guy's neck he jumped off the ladder so that his neck broke. He was dead when they cut him open – and the executioner was dead disappointed.

The English people were so shocked at the thought of losing their new king that James became more popular than ever ... and the Catholics more hated and feared. Or was that what James wanted? A Catholic visitor to England in 1605 said...

 Some people are sure that this was a trap. The government tricked these men.

So, did slimy James 'set up' Guy Fawkes to be caught?

Did you know...?
James spent a lot of money on rich clothes, but he had no use for the magnificent jewelled dresses of Queen Elizabeth I. The Master of the Wardrobe sold over 1,000 of them and made himself a fortune!

Curious cures

Stuart medicine was a mixture of the clever and the crazy. *Clever* William Harvey discovered that blood 'circulates' – that is to say it goes from the heart, round the body, back to the heart and off again. Harvey discovered this by cutting up corpses, of course. He was so used to dead bodies that he wasn't bothered when he saw so many victims after the battle of Edgehill. In fact he sat under a hedge and read a book to pass the time. Then he grew cold ... so he pulled a corpse over him to keep warm.

MMM, I STILL FEEL A BIT CHILLY

POW
BANG

Before Harvey's discovery people knew that blood moved, but they thought it went backwards and forwards like a Yo-Yo. At the same time some *crazy* doctors still believed that a good way of curing someone was to let a lot of that blood out of the body. They tried this for almost every illness known.

Similarly, people couldn't agree about the effects of smoking. Most people know about James I's hatred of smoking. He said smoking was...

...a custom loathsome to the eye, hateful to the nose, harmful to the brain, dangerous to the lungs, and in the black stinking fumes it resembles the smoke of the pit that is bottomless [Hell].

James then put large taxes on tobacco to put people off smoking. *Clever* James I. But, while the king was writing those wise words, the smokers were pointing to crazy Nicholas Culpeper's *Complete Herbal* book of 1653, where he claimed that tobacco…

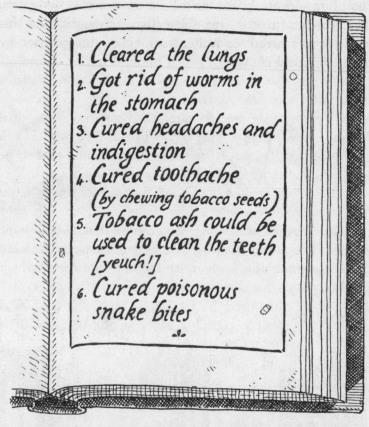

1. Cleared the lungs
2. Got rid of worms in the stomach
3. Cured headaches and indigestion
4. Cured toothache (by chewing tobacco seeds)
5. Tobacco ash could be used to clean the teeth [yeuch!]
6. Cured poisonous snake bites

He also claimed that rubbing tobacco juice into children's heads would kill lice in their hair.

Who would you rather believe? King James or Nicholas Culpeper?

Did you know...?

Sir Walter Raleigh was said to have brought tobacco to Britain. In 1994, anti-smoking campaigners said Raleigh was to blame for 300 deaths a week from smoking illnesses. Queen Elizabeth II was asked to take Sir Walter's knighthood from him – even though he'd been dead nearly 400 years. The Queen refused, saying, 'He suffered enough.' That was true. James I cured Sir Walter's smoking habit for good by having his head cut off.

A sick idea

Smallpox was a common disease in Stuart times. Many died from it – 1,500 smallpox deaths in London in 1659. If you recovered from the disease then your face would probably be scarred for life with marks left by the spots.

Children recovered better than adults. So what would you do if you heard someone nearby had smallpox? Take your child to visit them in the hope that the child would catch the disease! They were probably young enough to recover and could go through life without having to worry about it.

Find the cure!

Here are ten illnesses. If you were a Stuart doctor what would you prescribe? Match the cure to the illness ... just don't expect them to work and *don't* try them on your friends!

Illness I

1 Accidentally swallowing a snake (!) [Boot it out]
2 Heavy bleeding [This should make it all write]
3 Stopping yourself from becoming drunk [Make a pig of yourself]
4 Colic (stomach pains) [The cure shouldn't kill you stone dead]
5 Toothache [You'll be oak-kay after this]
6 Consumption (lung disease) [This should slip down nicely]
7 Fever [Coo—what a thought]
8 Accidentally swallowing a horse leech in drinking water [Make it flee]
9 Preventing the plague from infecting you [A rich food]
10 Jaundice (liver disease) [wear a clothes peg on your nose]

Cure

a Place a cold marble stone
(on which the sun has never
shone) on the stomach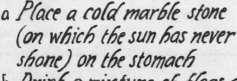

b Drink a mixture of fleas and vinegar

c Eat snails boiled in milk and a few
chopped worms if you wish

d Burn the sole of an old shoe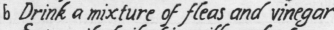
and breath in the smoke

e Place a gold coin in the mouth

f Write the word 'Veronica' on your left
thumb

g Take two 'tench' fish, split them open
and place them on the feet. Leave for
12 hours 'even if they begin to stink,'
then put fresh ones on

h Cut a pigeon in half and place one half
on each foot

i Scratch your gum with
a new nail then drive the
nail into an oak tree

j Eat the roasted lungs of a pig first
thing in the morning

Answers:

1 d) *R. Surflet, 1600.* He reckoned snakes could creep into farmers' mouths as they slept in the fields. He also swore the cure was 'tried and approved'.

2 f) *Madam Suzannah Avery, 1688.* She actually wrote a book with many sensible cures in. This wasn't one of them.

3 j) *John Goldsmith, 1678.* Other medicines included powdered berries of ivy dissolved in vinegar. After that you probably couldn't face drinking anything else!

4 a) *Traditional cure.* Probably helped soothe the pain! If you couldn't find a piece of marble then a lump of turf was supposed to work too. (If you want to try this, shake the worms out first.)

5 i) *J. Aubrey 1670.* He said, 'This cured William Neal's son when he was so mad with pain he was ready to shoot himself.'

6 c) *Traditional cure.* Stupid Stuarts? Well, this cure was made even slimier by the American settlers who brought it from Britain – they ate a *live* snail every morning for 9 days. And they were still doing it in 1929!

7 h) *Traditional cure.* No good for the fever sufferer. Worse for the pigeon!

8 b) *R. Surflet, 1600.* If you accidentally swallow a horse leech while drinking a glass of water it's probably your eyes that need seeing to!

9 e) *John Allin, 1665.* Doctor Allin said a coin with Queen Elizabeth's head on works best.

10 g) *J. Aubrey, 1670.* Don't *eat* the used fish – bury them or the cure won't work.

Charles I (reigned 1625-1649)

Ch-ch-ch-charlie

Charles I didn't really expect to be king. His older brother, Henry, was the first in line to the throne. But Henry fell ill. Doctors suggested a remedy of pigeons pecking at the bottom of his feet! Henry died – Charles was heir to the throne.

Charles was shy and nervous but tried hard to cover this up by acting strong. He had his father's Scottish accent and a squeaky little voice with a stammer. His eyes never rested on the people he was talking to, but seemed to look through them. Charles had few friends. He listened to his father's favourite adviser, Buckingham, and really let him run the country. But Buckingham was stabbed to death by a soldier. The soldier was upset because Buckingham hadn't given him the promotion he thought he deserved.

Charles's fatal friends

When Buckingham was murdered Charles grew closer to his wife, Henrietta Maria. The British people thought this was dangerous because she was a Catholic and they never really trusted her or liked her.

Charles also asked Thomas Wentworth, nicknamed 'Black Tom', for advice. Black Tom was hated for his brutal methods.

Charles's Archbishop of Canterbury, William Laud, gave Charles bad advice as well. Laud angered the Scots *and* the

Puritans with his orders... he wanted them to pray just like those dreaded Catholics! The Puritans entered Parliament and tried to bring in new laws.

Parliament raised an army ... so Charles raised an army. The King's army (the Royalists or Cavaliers) fought the army of Parliament (the Roundheads).

Slimiest acts

Slimy act 1: Parliament wanted Charlie's best pal, Black Tom, executed. Charles said he'd protect Black Tom. Within a week of making that promise, he signed Black Tom's death warrant.

Slimy act 2: When Charles started to lose the Civil War he made a secret deal with the Scots. They would send an army to help him. The Roundhead leader, Cromwell, was furious! He said this was treason to the English people ... and the punishment for treason should be death!

Charlie was one slimy Stuart who tried to be slimy once too often. He lost the war and Parliament sent him to be executed. That put a stop to his slimy games.

The execution of Charles

Charles stepped on to the scaffold and prepared to say those famous last words... but what were they?

As he took off his jewels and handed them to the bishop beside him he said, 'Remember!' Brilliant! What a dramatic last word! But, no. Charlie had to go and spoil it.

After a few moments of silent prayer he took off the cloak and put his neck on the block. The executioner brushed Charles's hair to the side to give him a clean cut.

Charles said, 'Wait for the sign.' *What a let-down.* 'Wait for the sign.' What sort of last words are they? They could be the last words of a policeman trying to stop a steam-roller at a crossroads.

Anyway, Charles stretched out an arm, the axe fell and severed the head cleanly. The crowd surged forward and some dipped handkerchiefs in the blood.

Did you know…?

After his execution Charles's head was sewn back on to his body so relatives could pay their last respects before he was buried. After Cromwell's death, however, *his* body was dug up and hanged, then thrown in a ditch!

Slimy Stuart riddle

The Scots hated Charles I's *Church of England Prayer Book* – but Scottish priests were ordered to use it. One Scottish bishop only dared to read it to his angry congregation if he held a loaded pistol in each hand. The Scots didn't want to be Church of England – they wanted to be *Presbyterians*.

Test your teacher with this old riddle: Presbyterians are said to be the most religious people. Why? (Clue: rearrange the letters of 'Presbyterians' to make a phrase of three words with four, two and seven letters.)

Answer: 'Best in prayers'.

The Civil War

A 'civil' war is where people in one country fight among themselves. They are usually especially slimy affairs. The English Civil War was no different. It had its fair share of comical and gruesome moments...

1 In The English Civil War (1642-1649), brother fought brother and sometimes groups of soldiers switched sides. Sir Faithful Fortescue's men changed sides – but they forgot to change the sashes they wore when fighting ... so their new allies shot them!

2 Sir Arthur Aston was not a nice man. When one of his soldiers committed a crime he ordered that the man's hand should be sawn off. But a year later Sir Arthur was showing off on his horse to impress some ladies. He fell off and broke his leg. It turned septic ... and had to be sawn off.

3 But that wasn't the end of Sir Arthur's punishment for his cruelty. He had a wooden leg fitted and boasted he was as good a fighter as any man with two legs. He wasn't. In 1649 his army was defeated by Cromwell at Drogheda in Ireland. A soldier caught Sir Arthur and beat his brains out. What did the soldier use to batter him? Sir Arthur's own wooden leg, of course.

4 Prince Rupert, the Royalist leader, took his white poodle, Boy, with him everywhere – including to his battles. The Roundheads were afraid of the dog's devilish powers. They said Boy could talk several languages and make himself invisible. They thought he also gave his master the power to be weapon-proof. Then, at the battle of Marston Moor, Boy wandered on to the battlefield and was killed.

5 King Charles's army suffered from having some dimwitted generals. In 1644 Lord Byron took charge of some fresh troops from Ireland and surrounded the Roundhead town of Nantwich. No Roundhead could get out of the town because Lord Byron's troops made a circle right round Nantwich even though the town was on the edge of a river! It was icy weather. The river was frozen. Brilliant Byron's troops could cross it when they liked. Surely Nantwich would surrender? But ... *the ice melted*. The troops across the river were cut off, and Byron's two half-armies were easily defeated. Just to make things worse, bird-brain Byron's fed-up Irish troops agreed to switch sides and fight with the Roundheads.

6 Lord Byron managed to do even *worse* at the next battle – Marston Moor, in Yorkshire. He sat with his horse-soldiers (cavalry) behind a deep ditch and rows of foot-soldiers with pikes. All he had to do was wait for the order and attack the Roundheads. Then he saw the Roundheads coming towards him. They would be slowed up by the ditch and battered by the pike men.

All he had to do was *wait*. He couldn't. He charged forward. First he *flattened* his own pike soldiers, then he got his own men tangled in their own ditches where the Roundheads were able to cut them to pieces. The battle was lost and with it the whole of northern England. All because Lord Byron couldn't wait.

7 The Cavalier leader, Prince Rupert, also came face to face with the Roundheads on Marston Moor, in 1644. By the time he reached the battlefield there was just an hour of daylight left. Hardly worth starting a battle now, he thought. So he ordered his men to stop and have supper. The Roundheads couldn't believe what they were seeing. While the Cavaliers were having a bite to eat the Roundheads attacked and massacred 3,000 of them. They fought on in the moonlight and by midnight the Cavaliers had lost the battle.

8 In 1643 a group of London women surrounded the Houses of Parliament shouting, 'Peace and the King.' They were asked to leave. They refused and started beating up Members of Parliament – especially the crop-haired Puritans. In the end the army was called in to drive them out. Three women were killed and many others locked in prison.

9 The Cavalier town of Colchester, Essex, was under siege in 1648. The siege went on for three months and the inhabitants were forced to eat cats and dogs. It got worse. When they heard that Cromwell was winning the war, they gave up. The leaders expected to be treated honourably as prisoners of war. The Roundheads took them to Colchester Castle and shot them. (Maybe they were cat-lovers.)

ANOTHER TIDDLES ON TOAST DEAR?

10 The Parliament forces had problems too. Beeston Castle was left in the care of a Parliament commander whose peace-time work was selling cheese. One night a Cavalier officer and eight men climbed the rock that the castle was built upon and crept into the castle. The cheese-seller was so shocked he surrendered his 60 men ... and then invited the attackers to supper and a drink of beer. When the angry Roundheads caught up with the cowardly cheese-seller, they shot him.

The spooky Stuarts

The stuffed chicken's revenge
Francis Bacon was a great statesman in the days of James I.
(No jokes about his name, please.)

Then he got involved in a scandal and had to give up
government work. Instead he turned his great brain to
solving the problems of the world. (Sir Francis was an expert
on manure, among other things.)

The problem of preserving food was one that strained his
brain for a while. Then, as he was riding through London
one snowy March day, he noticed that the frozen grass in
the tracks was as fresh as ever. 'Aha!' he thought. 'Maybe the
cold is preserving the grass. I wonder if it would preserve
meat the same way?'

He ordered the coachman to stop the carriage at the
nearest farm. He jumped out and bought a chicken. The
coachman was ordered to kill the chicken, to pluck out most
of its feathers and to clean out its insides. This he did.

Sir Francis bent down and began stuffing the chicken full
of snow. He then packed it into a sack full of it.

But the cold was too much for 65-year-old Francis. He
started shivering and collapsed in the snow. Within a few
days he was as dead as the chicken.

Deader than the chicken, in fact. For the chicken wasn't

finished. It continues to haunt the place to this day. Half-stripped, it runs and flaps and shivers around Pond Square in London. Someone tried to catch it during World War Two but it disappeared into a brick wall. It was last reported in the 1970s. But that's not the only Stuart ghost story...

The Civil War soldier spooks

One of the Civil War battles was at Edgehill on October 23rd 1642. Charles claimed that he'd won – so did Cromwell!

Charles's nephew, Prince Rupert, led a charge of horse soldiers. It was a great success. They broke through the Roundhead lines and reached their supply wagons. But the nutty nephew didn't know what to do next. The Cavaliers spent some time plundering the supplies then decided to join the battle again. Unfortunately they were too late. Charles was already running away to Oxford.

Two months later some farm workers near Edgehill complained that they were disturbed at night by the charging of horses, the roar of cannon and the blowing of bugles. The villagers went to see what was happening ... and they saw the battle of Edgehill – again. And again. And again ... and again. Ghosts seemed to be acting out the battle every weekend.

Charles sent some of his officers to report and they saw the battle too. Charles's reporters had been at the original battle and recognized some of the ghostly soldiers. They saw Sir Edmund Verney who had been holding the king's flag until his hand was cut off – still holding the flagpole.

The ghostly battle can still be seen every year on October 23rd, it is said...

Chopped Charlie's last chance

Charles himself was visited by a ghost…

The terror of Tedworth

One of Britain's most famous ghost stories happened in Stuart times. It concerns the *Phantom Drummer of Tedworth*.

Magistrate John Mompasson was visiting the town of Ludgershall in Wiltshire when he heard the deafening sound of a drum.

'What's that horrible racket?' he asked.

'It's a beggar. He has a special licence to beg and to use that drum to attract attention,' his friend explained.

'Look, I know the magistrates round here. None of them would sign a licence like that. Fetch him here.'

So the beggar, William Drury, was brought before Mompasson and showed his licence. It was a very clumsy forgery. Drury went to prison but begged to be allowed to keep the drum. Mompasson refused. Drury escaped from the prison and the drum was sent to Mompasson's house.

For the next two years the house suffered terrible drumming noises. Then the ghost grew more violent...

- A bible was burnt.
- An unseen creature gnawed at the walls like a giant rat, purred like a cat and panted like a dog.
- Coins in a man's pocket turned black.
- Great staring eyes appeared in the darkness.
- The spirit attacked the local blacksmith with a pair of tongs

- A horse died of terror in its stable.
- Chamberpots were emptied into the children's beds.

Drury was arrested again for stealing a pig in Gloucester. He claimed it was his witch powers that were cursing Mompasson. So Drury was tried for witchcraft and sentenced to transportation overseas.

The haunting of Mompasson's house stopped. Drummer Drury was lucky. Twenty years earlier he would have been burnt at the stake as a witch.

Test your teacher

Is your teacher a historical brainbox or a hysterical bonehead? Test him/her/it with these simple true or false questions...

True or false?

1 In 1648 James II was a 14-year-old prince. His father had lost the Civil War and the young prince had to escape from England. To disguise himself he dressed as a servant with old clothes and a dirtied face.

2 Roundheads were called Roundheads because of the shape of their helmets.

3 Cavalier General, Prince Rupert, taught his dog to cock its leg every time someone said the name of the Roundhead leader, 'Pym'.

4 Charles I went to France to marry Henrietta.

5 The Earl of Berkshire committed suicide by shooting himself with a bow and arrow.

6 At some cattle markets men sold their wives.

7 Stuart boys wore petticoats until they were six years old.

8 In south-west England children were forbidden to smoke.

9 People believed that a dead person's tooth, worn as a necklace, prevented toothache.

10 Guy Fawkes was arrested and taken to King James's bedroom to be questioned.

Answers:

1 False. James dressed as a girl with a specially made dress. The tailor who made the dress was given James's measurements. He said he'd never known a woman that shape before – but he made it anyway and it fitted. Anne Murray, who helped him, said 'he looked very pretty in it.'

2 False. It was the shape of their crop-haired heads that gave them their name. In fact many Cavalier soldiers wore the same helmets as the Roundheads and became so confused at times that they killed their own allies.

3 True. It also jumped happily in the air when he said 'Charles'.

4 False. He didn't go *anywhere* to marry her. He sent his friend, the Duke of Buckingham, who acted as Charlie's stand-in at the wedding in Notre Dame, France.

5 False. The Earl of Berkshire *did* commit suicide but he used a cross-bow and bolt. Easier than a longbow, but equally horrible.

6 True. This did happen from time to time. One husband was so pleased with the five guineas he got for his wife that he went to Stowmarket and ordered the church bells to be rung.

7 True. At the age of six they were 'breeched' – given their first pair of trousers – in a ceremony. They were also given a small sword to wear.

8 False. Children in Somerset, Devon and Cornwall actually took their clay pipes to school. Smoking was

considered healthy then. Pupils at Eton were ordered to smoke during the plague years because it was said to help you avoid the disease. The smell could well have sent the plague-rats packing.

9 True. Some people went into graveyards to dig skeletons up and pinch their teeth.

10 True. Knowing some of James's disgusting personal habits, a visit to his bedroom could have been nastier than a visit to the torture rack.

Teach your teacher ... Silly Stuart facts

Impress your teacher and get a wonderful report at the end of term. How? Approach teacher's chair/desk/cage and say 'I was reading a jolly good history book the other day and I learned some amazing facts...' then amaze/entertain/sicken your teacher with these intriguing tales. (One each day for a week should do the trick).

• Here's a sad thing... Off the coast of Cornwall is the dangerous Eddystone Rock. In 1693 Henry Winstanley built a lighthouse to warn ships away. The 26-candle lighthouse was built of rock and stone. Iron bars were sunk into the rock to keep it as firm as the Eddystone Rock itself. In 1703 a storm swept the lighthouse away. Winstanley may have been disappointed for a short while – a *very* short while. He was inside it at the time and disappeared with his invention.

• Here's a weird thing... The people of Caernarvon in Wales were desperate for a ferry boat to carry them across their river. They were so desperate that they pinched the wood from Llanddwyn church to build the boat. 'God will be angry,' the villagers of Llanddwyn said. 'So what?' the boat-builders replied. So ... the ferry sank in 1664 and 79 people drowned. 'Told you so,' taunted the villagers of Llanddwyn.

• Here's a curious thing... Some Stuart tramps made money by performing marriage ceremonies for couples. They called themselves Strollers' Priests. The marriage was made by the bride and groom shaking hands over the corpse of a dead horse.

HE'S NOT DEAD YET, BUT HE HASN'T GOT LONG TO GO

These marriages were not legal, of course.

• Here's a nasty thing... During the Civil War the soldiers used simple muskets - pour the powder down the barrel, put the lead shot in, light the powder: 'Bang!' Or, sometimes, 'Bang ... ouch!' Because accidents were common. As one Royalist officer said, 'We bury more toes and fingers than we do men.'

• Here's a horribly historical thing... An essential substance in gunpowder was 'saltpetre'. This was made from bird-droppings and human urine. Government officers had the right to dig these ingredients from hen-houses and toilet. In 1638 'saltpetre men' tried to get permission to go into churches to collect material because, 'women pee in their seats which causes excellent saltpetre.' (It must have been those long, long, sermons!)

Remember, remember...

Remember, remember the 30th of January! Charles I is remembered by some Church of England churches which have been named after him. Charles is remembered as a martyr who died for his religion. Charles churches can be found in Tunbridge Wells, Falmouth and Plymouth.

Remember, remember the 29th of May! It used to be Oak Apple Day and celebrations were held in remembrance of the Royal Oak... the tree that Charles II hid in to save his life. Oak Apple Day is now generally forgotten, but many towns now have a pub named after the Royal Oak – perhaps your town has.

Remember, remember the 3rd of September! On that day a small group of Oliver Cromwell supporters gather outside the Houses of Parliament. They sing a few hymns and a bugler plays a military tune of farewell, The Last Post. This marks the day of Cromwell's greatest victories (at Dunbar in 1650 and Worcester in 1651). It was also the day on which Cromwell died.

Remember, remember the 5th of November! James made this a public holiday when Guy Fawkes failed to blow up Parliament – 'Fawkes was the only man to enter the Houses of Parliament with an honest reason,' some people have said! But in 1678 there was a fear of another Catholic plot, so on November 5th people burned images of the Pope.

Sickly Stuart snacks

Would you like to have eaten like a Stuart? Like the Tudors before them, the rich people ate a lot of meat. They had servants to do the hard work of preparing it. Turning meat over an open fire was a hard job. It was usually given to a young kitchen boy whose front would be roasted by the fire, while his back would be chilled by the draught of the cool air drawn into the flames.

So the inventors of Stuart times came up with a couple of clever devices. One was a clockwork turner. The other was a sort of large 'hamster-wheel'. But instead of a hamster you popped a dog inside. As the dog walked forward, the meat turned.

The people of Stuart times not only invented new ways of cooking. They also discovered new food ideas...

The inventive Stuarts
Which of the following new food fads became popular in Stuart Britain?

Answers:

1 Yes. A Chinese legend says that Emperor Shennong learned how to make tea in 2737 BC when a few leaves from a tea plant accidentally fell into water he was boiling. A likely story. But it wasn't until the Stuart age that tea-drinking became popular in Britain. People of the 17th century thought it was quite all right to drink tea from the saucer. It took another 300 years (1920 to be exact) for someone to invent tea bags.

2 No. British politician John Montagu, fourth Earl of Sandwich (1718-1792), had a habit of eating beef between slices of toast so he could play cards without stopping to eat. But he was born *after* the Stuarts. And, though he gave his name to that type of food, the idea of eating meat between bread was first tried by the Romans over 1,000 years before.

3 No. Blame the Tudors for that. Sir Anthony Ashley of Dorset brought cabbages to Britain from Holland. (The stewed green mush you get for school dinners is not quite that old. Honest.)

4 Yes. Forks had been used on royal tables as early as the 14th century but only became popular when Thomas Coryat published a book about their use in Italy. Most people in Britain had used knives with sharp points to 'spear' their food and had spoons to scoop up the smaller pieces.

5 Yes. Oliver Cromwell was presented with a pineapple in 1657. The first in Britain. He probably didn't know whether to eat it, wear it or give it a bowl of milk.

6 Yes. Coffee was a popular Arab drink for hundreds of years before the Stuarts discovered it in the middle of the 17th Century.

7 Yes. From the early 1660s 'ice houses' with thatched roofs were built, or snow pits were dug in the ground. Winter snows were kept all year round. Sweet cream (sometimes with orange–flavoured water) was frozen for a couple of hours and then served.

8 Yes. Thomas Johnson showed bananas in his London shop window in 1633.

9 Yes. The Spanish brought chocolate back from Mexico in 1519. But it became really popular in Stuart Britain. In the 17th century, 'chocolate houses' were the popular meeting places of the day, rather like the local pub today. But you probably wouldn't have enjoyed the drink; it was full of cocoa butter and rather greasy. Some dealers added soil to the cocoa paste to cheat the buyers.

10 No. The Dutch first made eating chocolate in 1828.

Eat like a Stuart

If you were invited to eat at an upper-class house then you'd eat off fine silver and gold plates ... but you'd be expected to take your own spoon. Forks were not generally used until the reign of William and Mary at the end of the Stuart age.

Then Stuart people discovered how *really* useful forks could be. They found they were great for picking out bits of food that got stuck between your teeth!

And that wasn't their only habit that we'd find a bit disgusting today. They used their fingers a lot to pick up meat – and threw the bones on the floor for the dog. Everyone at the table used the same bowl to rinse their fingers in – and some people even rinsed their spoons in the same water.

One writer described a gentleman's country house in Dorset...

A house so badly kept that it shamed him and his dirty shoes. The great hall was scattered with marrow bones, it was full of hawks' perches, hounds, spaniels and terriers. The upper sides of the hall were hung with fox skins from this year's and last year's skinning. Here and there a polecat intermixed. Usually two of the great chairs in the parlour had litters of cats on them and the gentleman always had two or three accompanying him at the dinner table.

But some people worried about good table manners. A Stuart book gave advice on how to eat politely. Its top ten recommendations were…

If you wish to be POLITE at the DINNER TABLE

- Wipe not your greasy fingers upon the tablecloth
- Dip your food into the common salt dish before you eat it but not after you have taken a bite from it
- Bring not your cat to the dinner table
- Pick not your teeth with your fingers or your knife
- Make not a noise as you drink your soup
- Shout not at the table, 'I eat none of this, I eat none of that etc.'
- Blow not upon your soup to cool it
- Belch not at the table
- Spit not and cough not at the table
- Scratch not your head whilst you sit at the table

Fair gingerbread

People enjoyed going to fairs and eating. They didn't have candy-floss and hot dogs, though. Their favourite fair food was gingerbread. Some of the towns, like Birmingham, had Gingerbread Fairs. Want to know what gingerbread tasted like in Stuart times? Try this recipe.

Stuart Gingerbread

Ingredients
225g white breadcrumbs
5 ml ground ginger
5 ml cinnamon
5 ml aniseed
25 g sugar
150ml water

Instructions
1 Dry the breadcrumbs in an oven but don't let them turn brown
2 Mix the other ingredients in a saucepan and add the dried breadcrumbs
3 Warm gently and blend with a wooden spoon until you have a stiff dough
4 Dust a chopping board with ground ginger and cinnamon
5 Turn the dough out onto the board and roll it to about 5mm thickness
6 Cut into small circles (about 2-3 cm across)
Eat them without further cooking

Have a cup of tea (sugar but no milk) with your gingerbread for a truly Stuart snack. And, talking about eating…

Stuart food you may not want try

Stuart Christmas Pudding

Do you like Christmas Pudding? Most people do. You probably enjoy the candied peel, raisins, sugar and spices. So did the Stuarts. They were all in the Stuart pudding ... along with *chopped cow's tongue and chicken.* Fancy a spoonful?

Sweets

Decorate your table for that special occasion with sugar models. Make them into the shapes of animals and plants. Eat them to finish off the meal. Sir Hugh Platt described how to make the stuff in 1609:

Take violets and heat them with a little hard sugar. Steep them in rosewater and grind them into a paste. This will have the colour of the violet and smell of the violet. In the same way you may work with marigolds, cowslips, primroses or any other flower.

Eating flowers! Whatever next? Carnations and custard? Pansy pie? Baked buttercups and tulips on toast?

Charles II (reigned 1660-1685)

Cheerful Charlie

The leader of the Roundheads, Cromwell, died in 1658. His son wasn't very keen on running the country and the British people wanted a king again. So Charles I's son, Charles II, returned to the throne.

Charles II was known as the Merry Monarch because he brought back all the games and entertainments the Puritans had banned.

He wisely agreed to work along with Parliament in future. But Members of Parliament were still worried about a Catholic take-over – Charles was married to Catherine of Breganza, a Catholic princess from Portugal! Still, Charles himself was a good Protestant ... wasn't he?

Slimiest act

Parliament wanted to pass a law which banned any Catholic from ever becoming king - this was aimed at Charles's younger brother, James, who was a Catholic. Charles II was annoyed and sent Parliament away so the law couldn't be passed. He ruled without Parliament until his death in 1685... then James came to the throne as the royal family had planned.

But, slimiest of all, Charles II knew he couldn't be King of England *and* a Catholic - so he *pretended* to be a Protestant. Then, as he was dying, he told a Catholic priest he wanted to die a Catholic. He was 'converted' on his death-bed.

Charlie's cheerless childhood

In 1641 Charles I was forced to sign the death warrant for his friend, the Earl of Strafford. He wondered if Parliament might like to change its mind so he sent his son Charles to ask if they'd like to change Strafford's sentence to life imprisonment ... or, if they *had* to execute him, could they at least wait until Saturday, please?

Young Charles toddled off to Parliament with his dad's message ... he was just ten years old. The prince soon learned what a tough life it was. Parliament refused the plea and executed Strafford the next day.

Within a year little Charlie was involved in the Civil War and trying to take on a fully armed Roundhead with his pistol at the battle of Edgehill. He shouted 'I fear them not!' as the Roundhead charged ... but a Cavalier arrived just in time to save his royal bacon.

The Great Escape

In 1651, when Charles II was a prince, he was at the Battle of Worcester, fighting against the Roundheads. His army lost. He fled to a friendly house and was hunted by the Roundheads. Charles's friend, Colonel Carlis, led him to a huge oak tree. They climbed into it and the house owner took the ladder away. The king managed to sleep in the tree with a pillow he'd taken.

With the help of a haircut and a face blackened by soot, Charles escaped to Holland and safety.

Fire and plague

Londoners who lived through Charles II's reign were pretty lucky ... lucky that the plague didn't get them! And if the plague spared their lives then the Great Fire probably destroyed their houses. Would *you* have survived in Stuart London?

The plague ... read all about it!

 PLAGUE WEEKLY
9th Sept 1665
ON THE SPOTS REPORTS
Only 2OP WEEKLY

BOOZY BARD BEDEVILS BURIAL BOYS

Last night the brave burial boys, who collect your old corpses, were almost scared to death themselves. A strolling singer sat up and spooked them just as they were about to pop him in the pit.

Dirty

Corpse collector Samuel Simple (34 or 37) said, 'It's a dirty job but somebody has to do it. We was going along picking up bodies off the doorsteps where their loved ones had dumped them. We came across this scruffy little feller in a doorway. The door was marked with a red cross or we wouldn't have taken him. Stuck him on the cart

189

with the others and went off to the graveyard'.

His partner, Chris Cross (24-ish) added, 'We was just about to unload the cart when the bodies started moving, didn't they? Gave me a right turn, I can tell you. Turned out to be this singer trying to get out of the cart. What a mess. Bodies all over the place!'

Smelly

Wandering minstrel Elwiss Prestley, of no fixed abode, said 'I'd had a few jars of ale and just sat down for a nap. Woke up under this fat, smelly feller. Thought it was somebody trying to muscle in on my sleeping spot. Told him to get off, didn't I? Course he didn't reply... well, he wouldn't, him being dead like.'

Tonic

Sam and Chris were able to laugh about their grave mistake. 'We'll buy Elwiss a drink to make up for it,' Sam said. 'We can afford it – after all, business is good at the moment. They're dropping like flies.' Asked how he stays so fit and healthy Chris said he put it all down to 'Doctor Kurleus's Cureall Tonic'.

Doctor Kurleus Cures All

This is to give notice that John Kurleus, former physician to Charles I, offers a drink and pill that cures all sores, scabs, itch, scurfs, scurvies, leprosies and plagues be they ever so bad. There is no smoking or sweating or use of mercury or other dangerous and deadly substances. Doctor Kurleus sells the drink at three shillings to the quart and the pill one shilling a box. He lives at the Glass Lantern Tavern, Plough Yard in Grays Inn Lane

He gives his opinion for nothing

Plague pottiness

Doctors *said* that dogs and cats, pigs, pet rabbits and pigeons could spread the plague. The government believed them and tried to prevent the plague by killing all the dogs in the town. Dogs were banned from towns and dog-killers were appointed to round up strays.

Other doctors blamed dirty air – huge bonfires were lit in the hope that they would 'purify' it.

No one understood that the real enemy was the rats, whose fleas spread the plague. That fact wasn't discovered until 1898.

Other doctors offered miracle cures for the plague. They would also offer free treatment, as in the advert (above). There was a catch, of course. Doctor Kurleus would look at a plague victim and say, 'You need a quart of my medicine. That'll be three shillings please.'

'I thought your advert said you give your opinion for nothing!'

'I do,' the devious doctor would shrug. 'My *opinion* is free, the *drink* is three shillings.'

Sick people, afraid of dying a painful plague death, would give anything for a cure. The fake doctors grew rich and the people died anyway.

Dying to get to heaven

When there was no plague and families had time to bury their dead properly, the people of Stuart times had some curious customs. You may have thought burying corpses with money and belongings went out of fashion when Tutankhamun died. It didn't.

A 17th-century body was buried with...
• a coin (to pay St Peter at the gates of heaven)
• a candle (to light the way to heaven)
• a 10-centimetre layer of bran cereal on the bottom of the coffin (for comfort).

There was also a custom in some counties for families to hire a 'sin-eater'. This was a poor person who was given a loaf of bread to eat and a beer to drink... while standing over the corpse. The idea was the dead person's dead sins would enter the bread and be eaten – their ghost could then get into heaven.

Graves should have a headstone with a rhyme carved on to it. For example…

HERE LIES THE CARCASS
OF HONEST JOHN PARKHURST

Awful rhyme – but difficult with some surnames. What would you rhyme with your name?

Fire from France
This is the story usually told about the fire…

1 A little boy crept into Thomas Farriner's baker's shop in Pudding Lane. He reached up to steal a loaf that was cooling by the window. The baker swung round quickly. Too quickly – he scattered ashes over the wooden floor.

2 The shop caught fire. Soon the whole street of wooden houses was burning fiercely. Burning sparks spread the fire to the next street, and the next. It seemed half of London was ablaze.

3 When Charles heard of the problem he did two things...

MY ORDERS ARE TO BLOW UP HOUSES TO STOP THE SPREAD OF THE FIRE

YAY!

4 And then the King himself set off to join the fire-fighters. He ended up blackened by smoke and soaked with water... but won huge popularity with the people of London.

5 So did his final action...

YAY!

AND HERE IS A PURSE OF 100 GUINEAS FOR THE BRAVE FIRE-FIGHTERS!

That's the *heroic* story. Teachers never tell you the horrible historical *truth*. Did you know, for example, the people of London blamed French spies for starting the fire? Whenever they met a Frenchman in the street they would attack him.

A blacksmith met an innocent Frenchman walking down the street and struck him with an iron bar 'until the blood flowed in a plentiful stream down to his ankles.'

A crowd threw a French painter's furniture into the street then ripped his house to the ground. 'Maybe you'd like to set fire to it,' they said, 'just like you set fire to the rest of London!'

Several innocent foreigners were dragged in front of magistrates and charged with starting the fire. Then the son of a French watchmaker *confessed*! No one knows why. Farriner the baker (where the fire had started) said the watchmaker could not have got into the bakery to start the fire.

What did the magistrate do with this unfortunate Frenchman?

1 Deported him back to France.

2 Put him in jail so the mob couldn't take their revenge on him.

3 Set him free.

4 Hanged him anyway, if that's what he wanted!

James II (reigned 1685-1688)

Dim Jim

Charles II died without children so the crown passed to his brother, James II. But James was a *Catholic* and the people of Britain still had that fear and hatred of Catholics. The only thing that saved him was the fact that he had no son to take over after his death.

His daughter, Mary, was a good Protestant and husband William was the Dutch Protestant leader. When James died, Protestant Mary would lead the country. Things were fine ... until a 'son' suddenly and mysteriously appeared! Was this another slimy, sneaky Stuart plot?

Slimiest act – the warming-pan switch

James's wife, Mary of Modena, had five babies from 1672 till 1682 – and they all died. Then she was expecting another baby. When it arrived her doctor was miles away. Two nurses saw to the birth. To the horror of the British people it was a living boy! It would become another Catholic king! But a story went around...

- The two nurses had been paid the huge sum of £500 each – to keep them quiet?

- Mary's baby had died – but someone else's new-born baby boy was smuggled into the Queen's room!

- The baby was smuggled into the room in a warming-pan – a metal pan with a lid, usually filled with coals and used to warm a bed.

- The Queen's dead baby was smuggled out in the same pan.

Jamie's judge

Four months after James came to the throne there was a rebellion led by the Duke of Monmouth. The duke's rebel force was smashed at Sedgemoor, in Somerset, by James's troops. Monmouth was executed.

That wasn't good enough for James. He had all of Monmouth's supporters rounded up as well and sent to trial. He wanted revenge. He wanted to destroy, wipe out, annihilate, eradicate, exterminate, obliterate and mangle all opposition. He couldn't do that himself. He had to have some sort of trial – and some judge who would be as ruthless and rotten as necessary.

He chose Judge George Jeffreys. Good choice. He was described by the writer Violet Van Der Elst as follows…

Judge Jeffreys was known to have a very handsome face and at times would look almost kind and angelic. But there was no man living who had a blacker soul. Innocent men were hanged along with the guilty. There was the case of Charles Lindell. He said he had not left his shop – in fact he was arrested there. The night he was supposed to be out fighting with Monmouth he was sitting at home with his mother and sweetheart. All this he told to Judge Jeffreys. With his most kindly smile he listened and seemed to sympathize. Then his face twisted into a most horrible grimace as he turned to the poor prisoner, who had thought he had a good-hearted judge. He now realized the judge was a fiend, not a man. Judge Jeffreys told him he would be hanged by the neck, if not for taking part in the rebellion then for telling lies under oath. This man was only one of nearly two hundred that Judge

Jeffreys condemned to death. Another eight hundred were sentenced to transportation and slavery in the colonies – a slower but equally certain form of death.

WE'RE HEADING FOR A FATE WORSE THAN DEATH

WHAT'S THAT?

AMERICA

The trials were known as 'The Bloody Assizes' - no prizes for guessing why. The angelic judge did have a little soft spot for Lady Alice Lisle – he actually let her sit down during her trial because she was 70 years old. She was accused of sheltering rebels. She was found guilty and the thoughtful judge sentenced her to be burnt.

The executed rebels had their bodies preserved in tar. The bodies were then sent around the west of England as a warning to anyone else who thought of rebelling.

BUT, there was some Stuart justice ... after James II was finally overthrown in December 1688, Jeffreys was arrested; he died in the Tower of London.

Cowardy custard James

But did Dim Jim really expect to get away with the warming-pan trick? If he did then he was disappointed. Another Catholic king was more than the British could bear. They didn't wait for the baby to grow up and take over the throne.

Parliament invited Dim Jim's daughter, Mary, to take the throne with her very Protestant husband, William.

William landed in England – James ran off to Ireland. William's take-over was known as 'The Glorious Revolution'.

In 1690 James II tried to defend Ireland against William. He lost the Battle of the Boyne and retreated safely to Dublin. He met Lady Tyrconnel, an Irish noblewoman, in Dublin and complained...

Jim slipped away to France and safety.

Jim the brave
James wasn't afraid of fighting once he got into a battle. At the Battle of Lowestoft – a sea battle against the Dutch – he spent 18 hours on deck while sailors all around were being shot down. As the famous poet *didn't* say...

> *The king stood on the burning deck*
> *Till all the Dutch were beat,*
> *The crown of England on his head...*
> *And blisters on his feet*

Slimy Stuart crime

The Stuart age was one of the classic ages of the highwayman. Stage–coach journeys had begun. 'Stand and deliver! was the famous cry and the horse ride from London to York was the amazing achievement of one man ... but which one?

The great escape

But what was the great adventurer's name?
1 Dick Turnip (nicknamed Tricky Dicky)
2 William Nevison (nicknamed Swift Nicks)
3 Dick Turpin (nicknamed Dick Turpin)

You've probably heard the famous story about Dick Turpin riding from York to London to avoid being convicted of a robbery. Turpin *never made that ride*. A writer simply pinched the Nevison story and tacked it on to the Turpin tale.

Nevison met King Charles II, who gave him the nickname and a pardon. The Merry Monarch had a habit of doing that – even when the crime was one of the greatest in history…

Blood and the Jewels
Some people become famous because of what they do. And some become famous because of what is done to them. Talbot Edwards had that sort of fame. He lived to a good old age but never grew tired of telling people about the time he was robbed…

203

Old Talbot Edwards sat in the corner of the tavern and emptied his mug of ale. He ran a tongue over his toothless gums and enjoyed the flavour. Then he pushed the mug across the table to the young couple who sat opposite him. 'Another pint of ale will help my memory,' he smiled.

The young man signalled and the landlord brought a fresh jug to the table. Talbot dabbed at his watery eyes with a grubby handkerchief and reached for the ale. 'So you've heard about me, eh?'

'We have, Mr Edwards,' the young man said eagerly. 'I'm writing the story for a newspaper and wanted to hear your side of it.'

'It's ten years since the robbery,' Talbot shrugged. 'Why now?'

'Because Blood's dead,' the young woman put in.

The old man blinked and paused with his mug half way to his lips. 'Blood? Dead? No-o. Blood's not the sort of man to die. I just don't believe it.' He shook his head slowly.

'Tell me about him,' the young man urged.

Talbot Edwards sat back on the oak bench and half closed his eyes. 'Funny little feller, Colonel Blood. Ugly face with smallpox scars, short legs and brilliant blue eyes. Lovely Irish voice. He could talk the tail off a pig. I was in charge of the Tower of London back in 1671 when he turned up on my doorstep. He was dressed like a parson, and he *told* me he was a parson... so I believed him!'

'He was a soldier, though, wasn't he?' the young woman asked. 'Came to England to fight for Cromwell and the Roundheads?'

Old Talbot threw back his head and laughed. 'Bless you, no! He came to England to fight for the Cavaliers... he only switched sides to the Roundheads when he realized that King Charles was going to lose!' He chuckled and supped his beer. 'Of course he wasn't too popular when Charles the Second came back to the throne. The new government took everything Tom Blood had.'

'That's when he decided on the robbery?' the reporter asked.

'Aye. But being Colonel Blood it couldn't be any ordinary robbery, could it? No. It had to be the most daring robbery of all time. He had to go for the Crown Jewels, didn't he.'

'And it was your job to guard them?' the young woman asked.

'I was the keeper. Lived on the floor above the jewel room. Of course, my job was to show visitors the jewels – especially *respectable* visitors like 'Parson' Blood. And I never suspected a thing. He spent months setting it up, you see. Brought his wife with him on the second visit. I remember she took ill

205

in the jewel room and my wife Nell looked after her. Parson Blood was so grateful he came back two days later with a pair of new gloves for Nell. After that he became a sort of friend of the family.'

'And he didn't show an unusual interest in the jewels?'

'No-o. He seemed more interested in making a match between his rich nephew and my daughter. Of course the women were keen on that!' old Talbot said.

'So how did the robbery happen?' the reporter asked.

'I'm coming to that,' the old man said and took a long drink of his ale. 'Parson Blood brought his good-looking nephew to meet Nell and Alice – that's my daughter – and he brought a couple of friends along too. "Now we don't want to be bothered with this marriage business, Talbot, do we?" Blood says. "No," I says. "Why don't we take my two friends here down for a look at the jewels while the women have a chat?" And I agreed.'

'And that's when he tried to steal the jewels?' the young woman asked.

'I'm coming to that,' Talbot Edwards said. 'Being a private visit I didn't have any of the Tower guards around, did I? So, there I was, alone in the jewel room with three villains. No sooner had I unlocked the door than Blood gave me a whack over the head with a wooden mallet. When I woke up they'd already pulled away the iron grating and were pulling out the crown, the sceptre and the orb. A hundred thousand pounds' worth of jewels ... what a robbery, what a man!'

'You sound as if you admired him,' the puzzled young woman said.

Old Talbot chuckled. 'Can't help it, can't help it. Anyway, when I woke up I found they'd tied my hands and feet. I started shouting, "Treason! Murder!" That's when Blood drew his sword and ran it through my shoulder ... lucky it missed my heart, really. Want to see the scar?' he asked and reached for the buttons on his doublet.

'No!' the young woman said quickly and turned up her small nose with a little show of disgust.

Talbot Edwards shrugged. 'That's when Blood had his one stroke of really bad luck. Like I said, it was a private visit so we shouldn't have been interrupted. They'd flattened the crown with the mallet and were stowing the jewels in a bag.

Who should arrive at the Tower? My own son. On leave from the army fighting in Holland. I wasn't expecting him – and Blood certainly wasn't. He made a run for it with his nephew and his two helpers. The blood was pouring out of my chest but I managed to shout out. My son heard and came and found me.'

The old man was becoming excited now and his watery eyes were glowing in the yellow light of the candles.

'Your son raised the alarm?'

'He did. A sentry tried to stop Blood ... so Blood shot him. The second sentry saw that and ducked. He let the robbers through the first door. There was a lot of confusion, you understand – guards were attacking each other by mistake. That let Blood reach his horse at the gate. But the Captain of the guard, a man called Beckman, saw what was happening and grabbed Blood just before he got on his horse. Blood pulled out a pistol, pulled the trigger ... and had his second bit of bad luck. The pistol misfired. Beckman wrestled him to the ground and the whole gang were arrested.'

The young woman leaned forward. 'What I don't understand is why didn't Blood hang for the crime?'

The old keeper shook his head. 'Didn't I tell you? Blood could charm milk from a bull. He insisted he had to talk to King Charles himself. In the end the king agreed to see him. Now, Blood knew the king liked an adventurous rogue. Sure enough, Charles pardoned him ... even gave him lands in Ireland worth £500 a year to make up for what he'd lost.'

'And the king gave *you* a reward,' the reporter said.

The old man looked into his empty ale mug a little shyly.

'A good king is Charles. I'd drink his health ... if I had a drink.'

The reporter smiled and signalled for the landlord to refill the old keeper's mug. After they had drunk the health of King Charles, Talbot Edwards sighed. 'So Tom Blood is dead, you say?'

The reporter nodded. 'I'm writing his story now. You know he'd just lost a court case to the Duke of Buckingham? The court ordered Blood to pay £10,000 to the duke. He was ruined.'

The old man looked up. 'So Colonel Blood came to a bad end after all,' he said.

The young woman spoke in a low voice so no one could overhear. 'There were stories that Blood had faked his death. That there was some other person's body in the coffin. The magistrates had it dug up and identified. It was Blood all right.'

Talbot Edwards looked disappointed. 'Trust Colonel Blood to cheat his enemies to the last.'

'Oh, but he didn't cheat them...' the woman began.

The old man cut in. 'He did, you know. Because he cheated them out of what they wanted most of all... what they really wanted was to see him hang!'

And in the smoky light of the tavern candles the old man chuckled so loud and long he could scarcely drink his ale.

Did you know...?

1 Colonel Blood was involved in many outrageous crimes in his lifetime. In 1660 he tried to capture Dublin Castle and hold its governor to ransom. When he failed he fled to Holland.

2 In 1661 one of Blood's partners in the Dublin Castle kidnap was taken to London for execution. Blood returned to England, overcame a guard of eight soldiers and rescued his friend.

3 Blood's greatest enemy was Lord Ormonde. One night Ormonde was on his way to a banquet when his coach was stopped by a band of armed men. They could have killed him on the spot but Blood wanted a more dramatic death for his enemy. He wanted him taken to Tyburn gallows and hanged like a common criminal. The coachman raised the alarm and the plot failed.

4 When Charles met Blood, the Colonel had the cheek to tell the king that the Crown Jewels weren't really worth that much. People said they were worth £100,000 – Blood said he wouldn't give £6,000 for them. Charles was amused and released the thief.

5 Not only did Blood get an Irish estate from Charles, he was also welcomed into the royal court where he was a popular figure. He was admired as the man who almost stole the Crown Jewels ... and Talbot Edwards was almost as famous as the man who almost lost them.

The teacher and the lord

Who would you rather marry, a lord or a teacher?

PERSONALLY I'D RATHER MARRY A *CHIMPANZEE* THAN A TEACHER

In 1709 a Scottish woman had the choice between Robert Lord Balfour of Burleigh and a teacher, Henry Stenhouse.

SHE CHOSE LORD BALFOUR OF COURSE

She chose the *teacher*. Lord Balfour was furious. He decided to sort Henry the teacher out. He killed him. Lord Balfour was arrested.

CRUELTY TO ANIMALS I SUPPOSE

Arrested for *murder*, found guilty and sentenced.

KILLING A TEACHER? DESERVES AN HOUR'S DETENTION AT THE MOST

Lord Balfour was sentenced to *death*. He was thrown into prison and waited to be executed. When the warders came to lead him to the scaffold they found he'd gone. Lord Balfour had swapped clothes with his sister when she came to visit. He walked free. Of course the poor woman married neither of the men.

SAD. STILL IT COULD HAVE BEEN WORSE... SHE COULD HAVE MARRIED THE TEACHER!

Before Stuart times lords expected to get away with murder. James I put an end to that when he ordered the execution of Lord Maxwell for murder in 1613. Maxwell had called a peace conference with his ancient enemy, John Johnstone. When Johnstone arrived at the meeting place, Maxwell shot him. Maxwell expected James to pardon him because he was a lord. James didn't. Maxwell was beheaded ... and the other lords were a bit more careful about who they murdered in future.

The Archbishop of Canterbury, on the other hand, *did* get away with murder. He was out hunting for deer when he carelessly shot one of his gamekeepers with a crossbow. King James I was told of the tragedy. 'Ah, well,' the king sighed, 'No one but a fool or a villain could blame the Archbishop. It could happen to anyone.' The Archbishop went free.

Painful punishments

1 Sir Walter Raleigh had been a hero in the days of old Queen Elizabeth. But he'd been accused of plotting against James I and was sentenced to death on the scaffold in 1603. James decided not to execute Raleigh – he thought he'd just lock him up instead. But James had to have his little joke. First he let Raleigh grovel for his life, then he let Raleigh climb on to the scaffold. The crowd held its breath and looked forward to a bit of blood splashing around. Only *then* did James let him know his life was spared.

After 13 years in jail he was released to seek gold in America. But Raleigh had upset the Spanish king, who demanded that James should execute him. James didn't have a very good reason to execute the old man – so he dug up the old 'plot' accusation from 1603. In 1618 Raleigh's head rested on the block for a second time. If he thought James was going to have another little joke he was disappointed. This time – 15 years after he'd first put his head on the block – it hit the ground.

2 The Duke of Monmouth led a rebellion against James II in 1685 but was defeated and captured. On the scaffold he tested the edge of the axe and said he thought it was a little blunt. The Duke offered the executioner, Jack Ketch, six gold guineas to do a quick, clean job. But the Duke was cooler than Ketch, who took about five chops to get the head off. The crowd was furious and Ketch had to be protected from them as he left.

3 They didn't have that problem in Halifax. They had a machine there to execute people. It was a guillotine. The blade was released by pulling on a rope. That rope was

passed to the crowd so everyone pulled together. That way no single person was to blame for the criminal's death. If the criminal had stolen an animal then it was tied to the rope and driven away. So a cow could guillotine a man!

4 A Scottish law said that people could be sentenced to drowning in the sea if they refused to support the Scottish church. No one believed the old law would ever be used again. But it was, in 1685. Sixty-year-old Margaret McLauchlan and 18-year-old Margaret Wilson were tied to stakes at low tide. As the tide rose the sea would drown them. The old woman was placed lower in the water. The officers hoped she would die first and the sight would persuade young Margaret to change her religion. It didn't. Old Margaret drowned and a soldier put young Margaret out of her misery by forcing her head under the water.

5 Scotland wasn't a healthy place to be at that time. In 1691 the Scots chiefs were told to take an oath to show they were loyal to King William III. But they had to take that oath before January 1st 1692. Alisdair McIain, head of the Macdonald clan, went to Fort William to take the oath. He was told to go to Inverary, 60 miles away. He battled through snow storms and arrived six days too late.

That was enough for the Scottish secretary to order the killing of all the Macdonalds. Thirty-five men and an unknown number of women and children died when the commander of the Argyll regiment, Robert Campbell, ordered his men to massacre the defenceless Macdonalds in their village at Glencoe. To this day the Macdonalds and the Campbells are said to distrust each other.

6 The Puritans brought in new laws after they had won the Civil War. Puritan punishments included:

CRIME	PURITAN PUNISHMENT
A man disagreed with the Puritan religion	Soldiers sold his furniture sent his servants to London and dug up every tree in his orchard
A woman swore [seven rude words]	Fined 12 shillings [60°]
A barber trimmed someone's beard on a Sunday	Fined
A man stole lead from a house roof	Whipped for two hours 'till his body be bloody' and sent to prison till a fine was paid
Being actors in a travelling theatre company	Whipped and sat in stocks
A maid mended a dress on Sunday	Sat in the stocks for three hours
People went to church on Christmas Day	Sent to prison

The poet Richard Brathwaite wrote…

> *One day to Banbury I came*
> *And there I saw a Puritane*
> *Hanging of his cat on Monday*
> *Cos it killed a mouse on Sunday*

(Mr Brathwaite wrote that in 1638, of course. He wouldn't have dared to write that 12 years later when the Puritans were running the country!)

No wonder the people were pleased to see Charles II return. He really seemed to be a 'Merry Monarch' – but after the Puritan reign, a game of chess with a chimpanzee would have seemed a 'merry' idea.

7 An actor called Wilson played the part of 'Bottom' in Shakespeare's *Midsummer Night's Dream*. He had to dress as an ass for part of the play. The magistrates must have had a sense of humour. While Wilson sat in the stocks he wore a label round his neck saying…

> *Good people, I have played the beast,*
> *And brought bad things to pass.*
> *I was a man, but now I've made*
> *Myself a silly ass!*

I DON'T KNOW WHAT'S WORSE, THE STOCKS OR THE POETRY

8 A man called Titus Oates was sentenced to be tied to the back of a cart as it was driven from Aldgate to Newgate. As he was dragged along he was whipped. King James ordered that the treatment should be repeated on a second day. Oates was too weak to walk – he was fastened face down on a stretcher and dragged through the streets again being whipped. And Oates was lucky ... he deserved worse! His crime was that he had dreamed up a story about a Catholic plot to murder Charles II. The country was thrown into a panic and innocent Catholics were tortured, executed or driven out of their homes by frightened Protestants. Oates claimed the Catholics had invited a French army to invade, and...

- An army was reported to have landed one night in Dorset
  – but in daylight the French soldiers turned out to be a hedge and their officers a few grazing horses.
- Chains were thrown across London streets to stop French cavalry charging.
- Tailors started selling 'armour' to rich men and women. It became very fashionable because it was silk armour.

9 William Prynne was a Member of Parliament and simply hated the theatre. He wrote a strong attack on plays and actors. Charles I on the other hand loved the theatre. So Charles had Prynne punished for his writing. Prynne had both ears cut off.

Five years later Prynne was writing nasty things about bishops. This time a judge said…

…*and* he pointed to a pair of stubs. These were cut off and he was branded on the cheeks.

William Prynne lived to see Charles II come to the throne – and Charles gave him a well-paid job in the Tower of London.

10 The dreadful Judge Jeffreys was especially thoughtful at Christmas time. He once sentenced a woman to be whipped but kindly added an instruction to the man with the whip, 'Pay particular attention to this lady. Beat her soundly till the blood runs down. It is Christmas, a cold time for madam to strip. See that you "warm" her shoulders thoroughly.'

11 When the Roundheads captured a Scottish Cavalier they put him in the stocks. They then held his mouth open with two sticks, pulled his tongue out to its full length and tied two sticks to it. The man couldn't pull his tongue back in. He had to stay like that for half an hour.

12 Not many people know that James I was a detective. True! A servant called Sarah Swarton said she had witnessed Lord Roos taking part in some hanky-panky with a woman who wasn't his wife. She said she'd hidden behind a window curtain in his Wimbledon home. Lady Roos went to King James to complain and have her husband punished. 'Sherlock' James went to the scene of the crime and asked the maid Sarah to stand behind the curtains. The curtains only came to her knees. She couldn't have stood there without being seen! Lord Roos was cleared – false-witness Sarah was charged with 'perjury', or lying after swearing to tell the truth. She was punished by being whipped then branded – she would probably have had the letter 'P' for perjurer burned into her cheek.

Potted punishments

Can you match the name of the Stuart punishment to its description?

NAME	DESCRIPTION The victim...
Branks	1. had his thumbs placed in a vice which was tightened until he talked
Repentance stool	2. was placed in a barrel with a hole in the top and bottom [For head and legs] and a hole in each side for the arms. Victim walked round street dressed in barrel
Cropping	3. had to wear an iron mask with a spike that went into the mouth. She then walked around the town wearing it. A punishment for women who nagged or talked too much

Drunkard's cloak	4. sits down in church while the priest tells everyone what a disgusting person this is
Thumbekins	5. had his head put in a pillory and his ears nailed to the wood. The ears were then cut off and often left fastened to the pillory

William (reigned 1689-1702) and Mary (reigned 1689-1694)

Slimy Mary

Mary had no regrets about taking the throne from her own father, James II, when he ran away to France. In fact, when she arrived at her father's palace, she was so happy she ran through the bedrooms and bounced on all the beds. (Mary was a large woman – but there is no record of the damage to the beds)

Slimy William

William had a girlfriend called Betty Villiers. Mary's father, James II, tried to stir up trouble between the couple. He said his spies had found out all about Betty Villiers – what was she going to do about it?

What she decided to do was have a very sharp word with William. But Willy used weasel words to worm his way out of it. 'I swear to you by all that is most sacred that I've done nothing wrong!' he lied.

Mary, the mug, believed him.

William sacked the spying servants ... and went on seeing Betty Villiers.

223

Dreadful deaths

Mary died in 1694 from smallpox. She was only 32 years old.

William died eight years later after falling off his horse. The horse stumbled on a mole hill.

He broke his collar bone and his surgeon 'set' it. He'd probably have recovered but he stupidly chose to return to Kensington Palace that evening. The coach ride was long and the Stuart roads rough. The broken bone was jerked out of place. This time it didn't heal and an infection eventually killed him. He died despite some incredible medicines ... like powdered crabs' eyes!

The supporters of James II (who wanted the old king back) were thrilled. Over the years they drank many toasts to the mole that dug that hole.

Slimy Stuart facts

Are you a mastermind or a mug? Answer these questions *without cheating and looking at the answers first*! Score five or more and you're a Stuart Mastermind.

1 What souvenir could you buy at the coronation of Charles II?
a) A slice of coronation cake.
b) A coronation mug.
c) A piece of Charles's coronation robe.

2 Samuel Pepys wrote a famous diary in the middle of the Stuart period. What did he write with?
a) A fountain pen.
b) A typewriter.
c) The feather of a mongoose.

3 What would you do with a 'lobster tail pot'?
a) Eat it.
b) Go fishing with it.
c) Wear it.

4 How much would you expect to pay a well–trained maid in the middle of the 17th century?
a) Two pounds a year.
b) Twenty pounds a year.
c) A hundred pounds a year.

5 When Queen Henrietta first saw her baby Charles (later Charles II) what were her first words?
a) 'He looks just like his father.'
b) 'He is so beautiful I am quite, quite proud of him.'
c) 'He is so ugly I am ashamed of him.'

6 What was the London speed limit for coach drivers set in 1635?

a) Thirty miles an hour.

b) Three miles an hour.

c) Twelve miles an hour.

7 A well-known cure for measles was to go to bed with…

a) A warm drink of rum.

b) A warm brick.

c) A warm sheep.

I'M NOT TAKING ANY CHANCES

8 At the siege of Basing House the Roundheads ran out of bullets. What did they do?

a) Made new ones from lead coffins dug up from the local graveyard.

b) Made new ones from lead off the church roof.

c) They picked up Cavalier bullets and fired them back.

9 Where would rich Stuart people get false teeth from?

a) Carpenters made wooden ones.

b) Potters made china ones.

c) Poor people sold their good ones.

10 The Stuarts had some strange names for their dance tunes. Which of these is NOT a Stuart dance tune?

a) *An Old Man's A Bed Full Of Bones*

b) *Punk's Delight*

c) *My Lady's a Wild Flying Dove*

Answers:

1 b) They were the first coronation souvenirs sold in Britain.

2 a) The fountain-pen didn't work too well and most people stuck with the old quill pen for another 200 years, but Pepys did use one of the first fountain pens from time to time.

3 c) The lobster pot was the name given to the Roundheads' helmets because of their curious shape. The neck guard was like a lobster's tail.

4 a) A manservant would earn double what a maid could earn. A steward (the head servant) who ran a large house for its owner would expect £20 and the Earl of Bedford paid his steward the huge sum of £40 a year.

5 c) Later, Charles grew up to agree with her. 'Odds fish, I am an ugly fellow,' he claimed. He said it!

6 b) Of course there were no policemen with speed traps – but if a coach overtook a walking law–officer he could face a fine.

7 c) 'Sheep,' Stuart doctors said, 'are easily infected with measles and draw the sickness to themselves, by which means some ease may happen to the sick person.'

8 a) They scattered a lot of bones around but thoughtfully chalked the names of the dead on the wall so they would not be forgotten.

9 c) 'If a gentleman has lost his teeth there are dentists who will insert into his gums teeth pulled from the jaws of poor youths.' - *Advert*, 1660

10 c) This is a 1960's pop song. A 'punk' in Stuart times was a wild woman. a) and b) are genuine Stuart dance tunes and other titles included *Petticoat Wag* and *Dusty my dear*. Scotland had the delightful, *The Lamb's Wind*.

Stuart women and children

Women have had a pretty hard time in many eras of history. But some modern historians believe that Stuart women weren't too badly off – compared to the Tudor women who lived before them or the Georgians who came after them. Stuart women had the usual problems of staying beautiful, of course...

Ten beastly ways to beauty

Stuart Superwoman April 1664

Beauty Tips
PAGE
editor

Girls! Do *you* want to look special for that man in your life? Here are the top ten tips from our Beauty Editor, Patricia Pasteface.

I Hair flair – want to have those lovely locks glowing like gold? Then why not try washing them in rhubarb juice and white wine? If you prefer to be a red-head then dye it with radish and leaves from a privet hedge.

2 Silky skin – don't let spots spoil that special date. If you have spots then why not try rubbing in the blood of: a freshly killed cockerel or a pigeon? (But, girls, don't forget to wash the blood off before you leave the house!)

3 Pale complexion – we know men love that pale and interesting look. If you have a weather-beaten face then burn the jaw bone of a pig and grind it to a powder. Mix with poppy oil and rub it into the skin. It'll turn as pale and pink as that pig in no time. Of course every woman wears chicken-skin gloves at night to keep those fair hands soft and white.

4 Sparkling eyes – spread a cloth on the grass on any night in the month of May. In the morning it will be soaked with dew. Wring out the dew and collect it in bottles. A quick rinse will make sore red eyes as good as new. But remember, only *May* dew will do.

5 Body beautiful – soak for two or three hours in a bath that's waist deep. Fill the bath with three gallons of milk then stir in a boiled mixture of violet petals, rosemary, fennel, mallow and nettles. Step out of the bath then go to bed and sweat, being careful not to catch a cold.

6 Farewell to foul freckles – wash those ugly freckles away with water of strawberries or the juice from watercress.

7 Dental delight – take the herb rosemary and the alum flower and burn them. Clean your teeth with the ashes for that sweet, sweet smile. And remember ... sleeping with your mouth open helps keep teeth white.

8 Rout the wrinkles – if your face has more creases than a cockerel's crest then wash them away with a mixture of elder flowers, irises, mallows and bean blossom.

9 In tune with the moon – wash your face in the weeks when the moon is growing smaller. Use a sponge morning and night in those two weeks and your beauty's guaranteed.

10 Teen queen – stay looking like a 15–year-old by washing in a mixture of eggs, asses milk and cinnamon spice.

These sound pretty useless treatments – but at least they were *harmless*. That's more than could be said for the gruesome Elizabethan make-up of a hundred years before. This had involved rubbing poisonous lead mixtures into the skin. And cleaning your teeth with ashes doesn't sound too tasty, but Stuart teeth were healthier than in most ages.

Of course, women were not only told they should be beautiful: they were also told how they should behave. You will notice that, as usual, it is a man who is telling them…

The English Housewife by Gevase Markham

THE NOTABLE HOUSEWIFE MUST…
· be brave
· be patient
· be tireless   WAAA!
· speak wisely…   A STITCH IN TIME SAVES NINE
· … but not too much   mmmmf
· be secret in her affairs   —DON'T SAY I TOLD YOU THIS BUT…

Witches

As in most other ages, most of the people accused of being witches in Stuart times were women. King James I was fascinated by witches. He believed there were several black-magic plots to kill him before he came to the English throne. He even wrote a book about witchcraft.

But the English were never quite as harsh towards witches as the Scots. A horrible history story from Victorian times could well be true...

The Witch of Irongray

'In the reign of James I, or in the early years of his son Charles's reign, there is a tale of a woman burned as a witch in the parish of Irongray in Scotland. In a little mud-walled cottage lived a poor woman who earned a little money by spinning wool and weaving stockings. She lived alone and was often seen on a summer's evening, sitting on a jagged rock above the Routing Stream.

Sometimes she would gather sticks, late on a November evening, among the rowan tree roots. Lying in her window she sometimes had a black-letter bible which had two brass clasps of a grotesque design to fasten it closed. When she went to church her lips were sometimes seen to be moving. She was known to forecast showers or sunshine at certain times and her forecasts were often right.

The Bishop of Galloway was urged to punish this woman for being a witch. He was afraid he'd be reported to the king if he failed to deal with her so he ordered her to be brought before him near to the Routing Stream. She was dragged roughly from her home. Several neighbours were called to declare the wicked things that she had done.

She was sentenced to be drowned in the Routing Stream. But the crowd insisted that she should be shut up in a tar barrel and thrown into the River Cluden. Unwillingly the bishop agreed. The wretched woman was enclosed in a barrel, fire was set to it and it was rolled in a blaze into the waters of the Cluden.'

The unlucky woman was Alice Mulholland. The English gave up hanging witches during the reign of James II and they didn't have any more witch trials after 1712. But the Scots went on persecuting witches a little longer. The last to be burned for witchcraft in Scotland was in 1722.

Women were still 'ducked' on a stool into freezing water if they nagged too much. That nasty habit went on until 1817 when Sarah Leeke was ducked. It all ended as a bit of a joke – when Sarah Leeke was ducked they couldn't get her under the water. The pool they'd chosen was too shallow!

Cheerless children

Would you like to have been a child in Stuart times? If you were the child of a strict Puritan then you could have started off life badly by being stuck with a rotten religious name. Which of the following nasty names were really given to nippers?

1. SILENCE
2. HELPLESS
3. FORSAKEN
4. MISERICORDIA
5. FIGHT-THE-GOOD-FIGHT-OF-FAITH
6. SORRY-FOR-SIN
7. GOOD-FOR-NOTHING
8. POSTHUMA
9. LAMENT
10. DISCIPLINE

Answer: All except number 7 were Stuart christening names.

The Puritans also had:
Kill-sin, Increase, Faint-not, Desire, Search-the-scriptures, Remember, Seek-wisdom, If-Christ-had-not-died-thou-hadst-been-damned, Safety-on-high.

There was also a name for those of us who have normal names - it was 'Be-thankful'!

Of course, you had to survive the christening ceremony in church. Stuart superstition said it was a good sign if the baby cried at its christening. That was a sign that the evil spirits were leaving it. Just to be on the safe side, the godparent holding the baby would give it a sharp nip to make it howl.

Toothy trouble

If you survived your christening then you still had to survive growing up. Many babies died because Stuart families didn't understand about germs. For every 100 people who died in Stuart times, 40 were under two years old.

Some rich parents couldn't be bothered with wailing and whingeing babies. They sent the baby away to nurses in the country until the child was old enough to walk and talk. They visited it from time to time.

Of course when a baby starts to cut its teeth it tends to cry a lot. The nurses had an answer. In *The Queen's Chest*, published in 1664, there was a little recipe for soothing those painful gums…

Boil the head of a hare. Mix the brains with honey and butter. Rub the mixture on the gums as often as you please

Switching schools

Would you like a school switch? Probably *not* if it was a Stuart school switch. Because a switch was a thin wooden stick and it was used to beat naughty boys ... girls didn't usually go to school.

Some people thought boys should have this thin 'switch' rather than the stiff wooden 'ferula'...

As for the ferula I wish it could be banned from schools. A good birch switch will not break bones or damage limbs. A good switch about the shoulders should be sufficient.

(Charles Hoole 1660)

Isn't that kind?

The rules of Chigwell school suggested...

Schoolmasters should not give more than three strokes of the rod at any one time. They should not strike any scholar upon the head or the cheek with their fist. They should not curse or swear at the pupils.

At least the Stuart pupils had one day every year when they could get their own back. Teachers handed power over to the pupils for a day and the pupils could use it to lock out the teacher - this was called 'Barring out'. Would you like to suggest it to your teachers? But there had to be rules, of course...

236

- The school master must know about it beforehand.
- The pupils must behave politely.
- Pupils must not use weapons to injure one another.
- Pupils must not damage the school.

Doesn't sound so much fun now, does it? In fact 'Barring-out day' sometimes got out of hand. In a Birmingham school in 1667 the governors complained...

> *Some of the scholars, being assisted by certain townsmen, did put into practice a violent exclusion of their master from the school. Though they deserted the school at about nine o'clock at night on the 27th November, some returned on 28th with unruly members of the town wearing masks and carrying pistols. Then they not only threatened to kill their school master but, for two hours, tried to break in. They threw stones and bricks at him through the window and broke through the walls of the school to endanger his life.*

That sounds a bit more lively, doesn't it? The report went on to say...

> *Some governors think the master should pardon the offending scholars. But they believe the people from the town who joined the riot should be punished by the law. Any pupil who attempts to exclude the master again should be expelled.*

So now you know. Getting the town toughs to attack your teacher is *not allowed*. Not even if teacher's a bit of a crook like the ones at Caistor School in 1631 where the school was *supposed* to be free and...

The schoolmasters are not to expect, demand or extract money for teaching any child, other than their wage.

But they did. The rich parents paid the school teacher *extra* money to give their children *extra* lessons. (Of course, nowadays your teachers are so well paid they wouldn't dream of taking extra money from your parents, would they?)

In 1673 Bathusa Makin opened a school for young ladies. She wrote that there would be more schools like hers but they wouldn't be popular with men. 'I expect to meet with many scoffs,' she said, 'because men would be ashamed of their ignorance.' In other words, brainy girls would show the boys up. (She could be right.)

Joyless jobs
Stuart boys would often be sent to learn a trade as an *apprentice* as soon as they left school. Their father would pay a skilled craftsman to teach his son a trade.

This was like another five to eight years of school ... only *worse* in some cases. A boy called Francis was sent to a scrivener for eight years to learn how to be a clerk. After three years he was suffering so much he wrote home to his father to complain. The letter may have gone something like this...

238

January 1643

Dear Dad

That's it I want to come home. Three years I've suffered here with old Bootley and I've had enough. There are three apprentices here and one of them is Bootley's own son. So guess who gets all the rotten jobs? That's right. Me

It's bad enough getting the boring copying to do, But you didn't tell me I'd have to slave in the house as well! Who cleans the boots before breakfast? Me. And who empties the ashes, fills the coal bucket, sweeps the shop, and cleans that nasty long sink? Me. I'm supposed to be learning to be a clerk!

Then Mrs Bootley uses me like a manservant. I'm in the middle of writing and what happens? The kitchen maid comes and orders me to fetch Mrs Bootley a farthing's worth of mustard or a pint of vinegar. Last week she sent me for a pint of beer, didn't like the taste, and sent me back to change it.

You paid old Boot-face thirty pounds for this. AND you paid him a hundred pounds for my good behaviour. If I make trouble you lose that hundred pounds. I know. So I daren't make a fuss. Just take me away from here! Your loving son

Frances

What happened to Francis after the letter was sent?

1 Francis's father complained to Mr Bootley and things got better.

2 Francis's father complained to Mr Bootley and Mr Bootley beat Francis with a cane...

3 Francis's father took his son away from Mr Bootley and lost his £130.

Answer: **2** Francis wrote... *I was little the better for writing to my father. No sooner had I come into my master's house than he went into his cupboard and fetched out a sturdy cane. 'By your leave,' or 'With your leave,' he lifts his sword arm like a fencer and gives me a lusty thwack across the shoulders. He said, 'I'll teach you to make complaints to your father.'*

Many masters *deliberately* treated their apprentices badly. They took a dozen apprentices at £50 each and made them so miserable that they ran away. The parents couldn't get the money back and the masters were hundreds of pounds richer.

Awful apprentices

The teenage apprentices often went around in gangs and were the 'problem' kids of their time. When the Puritans abolished holidays it was the London apprentices who went on strike to get them back.

In Tudor Newcastle there had been laws to stop them 'playing dice and cards, drinking, dancing and embracing 'women'. The older people thought the apprentices looked disgraceful with their silk-lined clothes, bearded faces and daggers at their belts: 'They are more like raging ruffians than decent apprentices.'

Fifty years later when James I came to the throne, nothing much had changed – except the apprentices had to find new ways to make trouble, and the old fogies had to find new ways to stop them.

A 1603 law said, 'Apprentices are forbidden to use any music by night or day in the streets. Nor shall they wear their hair long over their ears.'

Young people of today argue with their parents and their teachers about hair styles – perhaps you do! Then just be glad you didn't live in 17th-century Newcastle. Anyone found guilty of having long hair was...

• Sentenced to jail...
• *And* to having a basin put over the head and the hair chopped off along the edges!

University students had the same problem. In 1636 Edmund Verney went for his final exam with the head of his college. He wrote home to Dad, 'The head spoke to me very politely as he could not find fault with my hair, because I had cut it before I went to him.'

241

Battered bride

There was some sort of equality for women in Stuart times. Boys were beaten with sticks ... girls were beaten too!

Young Frances Coke didn't want to marry the rich John Villiers. John had occasional fits of madness when he might smash a glass in his hand and bleed all over the floor. Maybe Frances didn't fancy mopping up after him.

Her Father, Sir Edward Coke, said she *had* to marry John Villiers. There were 10,000 good reasons why she should – John was paying Sir Edward £10,000 for Frances's hand.

Frances ran away with her mother and hid. Sir Edward found the house, battered down the door and dragged the girl from the cupboard where she was hiding.

£10,000 FOR MY HAND? I WONDER WHAT THE REST OF ME IS WORTH?

'Marry John Villiers or else,' she was told.

'No,' she replied.

So she got the 'or else'. She was 'tied to the bedposts and whipped.'

She changed her mind – wouldn't you? – and finally agreed to marry the loathsome John Villiers.

Frances Coke was just fourteen years old at the time. Frances and John did not make a happy couple. She found a new boyfriend and ran off to live with him.

But it wasn't a happy ending. She lost her fortune to John Villiers's grasping family and she died in poverty.

Talk like a Stuart

Every age has its own slang. Are any of your schoolmates 'bagpipes' or 'barnacles?' (That's chatterboxes or hangers-on, of course.)

Do you have any 'muck in the sack of your kicks' at the moment? (That's money in the pocket of your trousers, if you hadn't guessed.)

Slimy Stuart villains

A book called *Leathermore's Advice* was published in 1666 and the writer complained…

Towards night there come Hectors, Trepanners, Guilts, Pads, Biters, Prigs, Divers, Lifters, Kid-Nappers, Vouchers, Mill-kens, Pymen, Decoys, Shop-lifters, Foilers, Bulkers, Droppers, Famblers, Dannakers, Crosbyters… generally known as Rooks.

You might not understand what he was writing about, but you get the picture. Stuart towns were not a safe place to be at night.

Why not amaze and impress your teacher/parent/gerbil by reciting this sad tale. They will certainly say, 'Well!/Gosh!/Eeeek!' … and then ask you to explain.

The fate of the fustilugs

There once was a fustilugs[1] slabberdegullion[2]
Who grew up quite buffle[3], not dossy.[4]
He learned how to mill-ben[5], to pug[6] and to dub[7]
Then this dunaker[8] jiggled[9] a hossy.[10]

But at budging[11] a beak[12] he was such a fopdoodle[13]
He was caught and sent down to the clink.[14]
'Oh the cage[15] belly-timber[16] is pannam[17] and old horse[18]
And we only get water to drink.'

1 a dirty eared child
2 a slob
3 stupid
4 brainy
5 break and enter houses
6 steal
7 pick locks
8 animal thief
9 rustled
10 horse – all right, this is *not* a Stuart slang word – but *you* try finding something to rhyme with 'dossy'
11 dodging
12 constable – later a judge
13 useless person
14 the name of a London prison
15 prison
16 food
17 bread
18 dried, salted beef

Beware the bung-napper![1]

If you wanted to survive in Stuart Britain you had to know who was out to get you. Can you match the criminals to their methods and their crimes?

THIS CRIMINAL	WOULD...	AND...
DARKMAN'S BUDGE	WAIT BY THE ROADSIDE	STEAL FROM YOUR HOUSE
SNOWDROPPER	HIDE IN YOUR HOUSE TILL DARK	ROB STAGE COACHES
SNUDGE	PLAY CARDS WITH YOU	LET A GANG INTO YOUR HOUSE
THIMBLE-RIGGER	CLIMB INTO YOUR HOUSE	STEAL YOUR WASHING
FOOTPAD	WALK PAST YOUR HEDGE	CHEAT YOU OUT OF MONEY

1 purse-snatcher

<table>
<tr><td>

Answers:

A **Darkman's budge** would climb into your house and let in a gang.

A **Snow dropper** would walk past your hedge and steal your washing.

A **Snudge** would hide in your house till dark and steal from it.

A **Thimble-rigger** would play cards with you and cheat you out of money.

A **Footpad** would wait by the roadside and rob stage coaches.

</td></tr>
</table>

And that's not all! A *sneaksman* was the lowest sort of thief. He just sort of lurked around and pinched anything he could get his hands on. A bit like next-door's cat.

- A *foist* would dip his hand into your pocket or purse while a *nip* would use a knife to cut a purse that hung from your belt. We'd call them pickpockets today.
- A *leatherhead* or a *ding boy* would simply beat you up and take your money – a bit like the school bully. (Note: It is *not* a good idea to call the school bully either of these names!)
- A *varnisher* would give you a fake coin – smartened up with (guess what?) a coat of varnish.
- Nothing was safe! Because you may find a *buffernapper* has pinched your dog or a *bleating cull* might snaffle your sheep. (Would we call him a *ram raider* today?)

246

Aren't you just glad you live in the 21st century where all you have to worry about are hackers (who don't use a hacksaw), twockers (who don't steal twocks), muggers (who aren't after your mug), armed robbers (who have three arms ... left-arm, right-arm and fire-arm) and serial killers...

I COULD MURDER A BOWL OF CORNFLAKES

Fox your friends
Say these two sentences to a friend then ask which of the two makes sense:

1. I'M NOT PLAYING MONOPOLY WITH YOU BECAUSE YOU USE A BRISTLE

2. DID YOU KNOW THE RIVER AVON RUNS THROUGH THE TOWN OF BRISTLE?

Answer: 1 A bristle was a dice that was 'loaded' to show any number the thrower wanted. It was used by slimy Stuart cheats.

Stuart fun and games

Fun at the fair

Stuart fairs were great holiday events. Lots of food ... and fighting. Lots of weird and wonderful entertainments. Can you picture this rope dancer from the description in the *Daily Courant* newspaper?

the Daily Courant

DANCERS ON A ROPE

At the Great Booth will be seen the famous company of rope dancers, the greatest performers of dancing on the low-rope, and walking on the slack and sloping rope. They are said to be the only amazing wonders in the world in every thing they do.

There you will see the Italian Scarramouch dancing on a rope. He has a wheel-barrow in front of him with two children and a dog in it. He also has a duck on his head who sings to the crowd and causes much laughter.

John Evelyn described a fire eater in his diary…

He devoured glowing coals before us, chewing and swallowing them. He melted a beer glass and ate it quite up. Then he take a live coal on his tongue and put on it a raw oyster. The coal was blown with bellows until it flamed and sparkled in his mouth. There it remained until the oyster was quite boiled. Then he melted tar and wax which he drank down as it flamed; I saw it flaming in his mouth a good while.

Slimy toads

If you lived in Stuart times you'd probably look forward to the annual fair in your area. Just like today's fairs there was magic, excitement and danger … and special food.

But would you like to eat a slithery, slimy *live* toad? Probably not. What about if someone offered you money to swallow that toad? Probably not. Because, not only would it be disgusting, it would probably kill you.

So one of the strangest sights at a Stuart fair would be the Mountebank. (A Mountebank was a man who called himself a doctor.) Imagine him going through the fair selling miracle cures…

'Ladies and gentlemen,' the Mountebank cries. 'Do you ever suffer from problems of digestion and distempers? Why suffer when you can try Doctor Cureall's Herbal Healing Tonic? This tonic is made from herbs to a secret and ancient recipe from ancient Egypt. It includes such rare ingredients as powdered mummy from an Egyptian pharaoh.'

'Rubbish!' someone calls from the crowd around him.

'Ah! We have a disbeliever, do we? Well, sir, what must I do to prove my miracle cure? I'll tell you what I'll do... I'll poison someone, then cure them!' the Mountebank smiles. He reaches into his black bag and pulls out a fat, warty toad. 'I have here a toad. Probably the most poisonous creature known to mankind. If anyone swallowed this then it would lead to almost certain death, would it not?'

There is a muttering amongst the crowd. They agree toads are poisonous.

'My miracle cure will defeat even the might of a toad's powerful poison. Now, can I have a volunteer to swallow this toad? Some brave person?' The Mountebank turns to the man who shouted 'Rubbish!' and offers it to him. The man turns his head away in disgust.

'Very well, I shall pay someone *six pence* if they will offer to swallow this deadly creature then be revived by my potion. No one? *Ten* pence, anyone? Very well I shall offer *one shilling* plus a free bottle of Doctor Cureall's Herbal Healing Tonic – which is worth a shilling itself. Do I have a volunteer?'

A shabby young man steps forward. 'I'll do it for a shilling,' he says.

'Ladies and gentlemen, a round of applause for this gallant young man.' The crowd claps. The noise of their clapping brings more fair visitors into the circle round the rough wooden stage. Everyone is hooked on this performance now.

Doctor Cureall pulls the stopper from a dark-blue bottle. 'I shall have the Herbal Healing Tonic ready to administer. But don't worry, young man, Doctor Cureall's tonic will work even if you are *dead*!'

The Mountebank passes the toad to the young man who looks at it nervously. 'One shilling,' Doctor Cureall promises, 'just for swallowing this creature.'

The scruffy young man closes his eyes, tilts back his head ... and quickly pushes the toad into his gaping mouth. He gives a huge swallow. The crowd gasps, and waits.

The volunteer's face begins to crease in pain. He gives a low moan and clutches at his stomach. His eyes begin to pop with the strain. He falls to his knees and cries, 'The cure! The cure!'

The Mountebank holds the bottle in the air, well out of the reach of the cringing young man. 'Shall I give him the cure?'

Someone laughs nervously, 'Let him die. Serve him right!'

But the young man screams in agony. 'Give him the cure,' someone shouts. Others join in, 'For God's sake, give him the cure!'

By now the young man is lying on the stage, rolling in agony. Doctor Cureall slowly reaches down and forces the bottle between the lips of the dying man. He drinks it greedily. Slowly his twisting body calms and he lies still on the stage. The crowd is silent.

The young man opens one eye. Then the other eye. He raises his head from the stage. He looks at his stomach with wonder and sits up. 'It's a miracle!' he cries. 'Here, Doctor Cureall, don't give me a shilling ... just give me another bottle of that Herbal Healing Tonic!' He jumps to his feet and clutches at his two free bottles as if they were liquid gold. The Mountebank turns to the crowd. 'Now, who else would like a bottle – only a shilling for a bottle of the secret of life itself!'

The crowd pushes and jostles to force money into the happy Mountebank's hand.

It is the end of the busy fair. And it is dark behind the Mountebank's stage. The doctor is counting his money when a by young man approaches. 'Have you had a good day, Doc?'

'Eight pounds and 16 shillings, my toady-eating friend. And here are your five shillings for your excellent job.'

The young man jingles the coins happily in his hand and turns to find a tavern to spend them in.

'I think you've forgotten something,' the Mountebank says sharply.

The young man grins a yellow-toothed grin. He reaches into his pocket and hands something over to Doctor Cureall.

A fat, warty toad.

Toad-eating facts

1 No one is quite sure how toad-eaters managed the trick. The young toad eater was probably a clever magician who *appeared* to eat a toad but never did.

2 When a toad is attacked it squeezes out a deadly milky poison. If the smell doesn't put off the attacker then the taste will. A dog trying to eat a toad will start foaming at the mouth and howling.

3 Even the Romans knew about toad poison. There is a record of Roman women using toad poison to kill their husbands. They threw the toad into boiling water and the poison rose to the surface. It was skimmed off and fed to the unlucky man.

4 Italian poisoners of Stuart times had learned to blend toad poison with salt.

5 Toad-eating was considered to be the lowest form of job. Clowns and jugglers at the fairs were more respected than a toad-eater.

6 A real creep will do anything for their boss, no matter how disgusting. So in Stuart times a new word was invented for creeps – 'toad-eater'.

7 Later the word changed to 'toady'. So instead of calling a pupil a 'teacher's pet' they would be called a 'toady' in Stuart times.

8 Some people swore they saw the toady swallow the toad. So, was it possible? There is just a chance that toad eaters really did swallow live toads ... and live. How? The toads could have been 'pets' who learned to trust their trainers. He might even allow them to sit on his tongue for a while so they didn't get excited by the idea and sweat poison. Then, on the day of the fair, he popped the happy toad on his tongue – and swallowed it quickly before the toad could react.

9 A young man who was fit, and who had just eaten a good meal, could probably survive a toad swallowing in this way. It could give him stomach and head pains, but he'd live.

10 A toady who wasn't fit could well die.

Next time someone offers you some sausage in a batter pudding, known as 'Toad in the Hole', you'll know what to say: 'Did I ever tell you about people who ate real toads...'

Eating toads wasn't the only fun you could have at a Stuart fair. There were prizes to win on the side shows and there were presents to take home for the family. Gifts to take home from the fair were known as 'fairings.' A popular fairing was a coloured ribbon.

There are many songs written about fairs. One of the most famous is 'O dear, what can the matter be?'

> *O dear, what can the matter be?*
> *Dear, dear, what can the matter be?*
> *O dear, what can the matter be?*
> *Johnny's so long at the fair.*

> *He promised to buy me a pair of sleeve buttons,*
> *A pair of new garters that cost him just tuppence,*
> *He promised he'd bring me a bunch of blue ribbons*
> *To tie up my bonny brown hair.*

But, did you know... young men would often go to the fair, drink too much beer and fall asleep. In the 1700s the navy 'Press Gang' would kidnap these sleeping young men and take them off to serve in the navy.

That could be why Johnny was so long at the fair ... he'd been press-ganged!

THE FAIR'S OVER LADDY, GET UP THAT RIGGING!

Sick Stuart sport

The Tudors, like Henry VIII and Elizabeth I, were supposed to live in cruel times, while the Stuarts are often thought of as 'modern'. The terrible truth is the Stuarts could be just as vicious as the Tudors ... or the Vikings for that matter! Here's a report from the end of the Stuart age. Make up your own mind about how 'modern' the Stuarts were from this report by a foreign visitor...

June 23, 1710

Towards evening we drove to see the bull-baiting, which is held here nearly every Monday in two places. On the morning of the day the bull, or any other creature that is to be baited is led round. It takes place in a large open space or courtyard, on two sides of which high benches have been made for the spectators. First - a young ox or bull was led in and fastened by a long rope to an iron ring in the middle of the yard; then about thirty dogs, two or three at a time, were let loose on him but he made short work of them, goring them and tossing them high in the air about the height of the first storey. Then amid shouts and yells the butchers to whom the dogs belonged sprang forward and caught their beasts right side up to break their fall. They had to keep hold of the dogs to hinder them from returning to the attack without barking. Several had such a grip of the bull's throat or ear that their mouths had to be forced open with poles

When the bull had stood it tolerably long, they brought out a small bear and tied him up in the same fashion. As soon as the dogs had at him he stood up on his hind legs and gave some terrific buffets; but if one of them got at his skin he rolled about in such a fashion that the dogs thought themselves lucky if they came out safe from beneath him.

But the most diverting and worst of all was a common little ass, who was brought out saddled with an ape on his back. As soon as a couple of dogs had been let loose on him he broke into a prodigious gallop – for he was free, not having been tied up like the other beasts – and he stamped and bit all around himself. The ape began to scream most terribly for fear of falling off. If the dogs came too near him, he seized them with his mouth and twirled them round shaking them so much that they howled prodigiously. Finally another bull appeared, on whom several crackers had been hung; when these were lit and several dogs let loose on him on a sudden, there was a monstrous hurly-burly. And thus was concluded this truly English sport, which vastly delights this nation but to me seemed nothing very special   Zacharius von Uffenbach

In 1760 bull-baiting was finally banned in Newcastle-upon-Tyne. A young sailor was gored in an accident. The 'sport' was banned because it was dangerous to the public, not because it was cruel to the animals!

Anne (reigned 1702–1714)

Anne was shy, stout, short-sighted and suffered from gout. In fact her gout was so painful that she had to be carried to her coronation!

She had 17 babies and 16 died. Only William survived infancy ... then *he* died at the age of 11.

Slimiest act

Would you betray your dear old dad? Anne did. Anne was Protestant and didn't want to follow her Catholic father, James II, during the 'Glorious Revolution'.

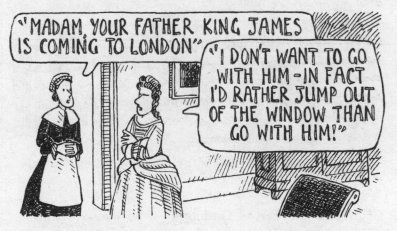

She didn't *exactly* 'jump out of the window' but she *did* make a secret escape at night down the back stairs. James went into exile and never sat on the throne again ... but Anne got her (very) fat bum on the throne 14 years later.

The Spiteful Stuart

Anne died in 1714 – she had grown so fat that when she died her coffin was almost square. Anne was the last of the Stuarts. Some said she was the *best*.

Her *friends* and *family* didn't say that.

Among the people she was spiteful towards were…

• Best friend Sarah Churchill – she was sent away when it suited the queen. Sarah was in tears, pleading for another chance. All Anne could reply was, 'Put it in writing'.

• Loyal adviser Earl of Godolphin – he was sacked. Anne didn't even tell him to his face. She just sent a message for him to snap his symbol of authority (a white staff) and get out.

• Her great army commander, Marlborough, who had won brilliant battles for her – he was sacked with a letter so nasty that he threw it into the fire and never spoke of it again.

260

• Her step-brother, James – Anne was quick to spread the rumour that he wasn't really her father's son; he was just a baby smuggled into the birth room in a warming pan. She then did an about-turn and tried to get baby James the throne when she died, instead of…

• Her successor George I – she knew his family would come to the throne of Britain when she died but she banned any of them from entering the country while she lived. Her main reason was simply that she disliked George.

For over 100 years her family had battled with Parliament. Anne brought peace by attending the House of Lords in person. She sat on the throne and listened to the debates – or in winter sat on a bench by the fire. When she died her doctor said, 'She welcomed death like a weary traveller welcomes sleep.'

Some Members of Parliament couldn't believe the news. 'She's not dead!' they tried to argue.

'Dead!' came the reply. 'She's as dead as Julius Caesar.'

Epilogue

Anne was as dead as Julius Caesar, but the Stuarts weren't quite as dead as a hedgehog squashed on the road. They kept trying to get that throne back. In the next 31 years the family of James II had a couple of attempts – 1715 and 1745 if you're really interested in dates.

A prince from Germany, George I, was invited to take over when Anne died. A new family sat on the throne the Hanovers. George I didn't speak English and never bothered to learn – he was especially cruel to his wife, whom he had locked up for 32 years.

IT'S A PITY SHE'S NOT AROUND

YES. AT LEAST SHE COULD TRANSLATE FOR HIM

The British people did not like George I. But they *didn't* support the Stuart attempts to get the throne back. Why not? Because they hated the slimy Stuarts *more* than the horrible Hanovers!

Kings had been overthrown (or over-throne) before in British history. They had been 'usurped' by powerful *lords*. But the Slimy Stuarts lost power to *the people*. And they didn't manage this once – they did it *twice*.

Now *that's* unpopularity for you. Quite simply, the Brits didn't want a Catholic monarch. The Stuarts kept *saying* they were Protestants – but acting like Catholics. That's sneaky and sly – slimy in fact.

Lots of innocent people died in civil war and revolutions during the reign of the Stuarts. Next time you light a firework on the fifth of November, look into the sparks and say to yourself...

Remember, remember the fifth of November,
Gunpowder treason and plot.
Was Guy Fawkes a devil, the Stuarts all saints?
Are we glad that they stopped him ... or not?

SLIMY STUARTS

GRISLY QUIZ

**Now find out if you're a
slimy Stuarts expert!**

Superstar Shakespeare

William Shakespeare used 17,677 different words in his writing. Amazingly, about 1,700 of those were new words! Can you spot the words (or phrases) first used by Shakespeare?

1. A place to stay is...
a) accommodation
b) a hotel
c) hard to find

2. If you're puzzled you say...
a) it's Greek to me
b) I don't understand
c) eh, you what?

3. If you're not mean you're...
a) kind
b) generous
c) sharing your chocolate biscuits

4. If you're unashamed you're...
a) open
b) barefaced
c) a nudist

5. To make someone go faster say...
a) quicken
b) hurry
c) little puff

6. A sudden wind is a...
a) blast
b) gust
c) little puff

7. A children's game is...
a) leapfrog
b) hopscotch
c) hopfrog

8. A reliable person is a...
a) tower of strength
b) brick
c) teacher

9. A person with no friends is...
a) lonely
b) friendless
c) smelly

10. Something that gets smaller…
a) dwindles
b) lessens
c) goes like a jumper in a hot wash

11. An lethal attack on a powerful person is…
a) murder
b) assassination
c) a bad idea

REMEMBER, REMEMBER...

Since the Gunpowder Plot was discovered it has passed into English history and is remembered every 5 November. But how many of these funny Fawkes facts are false?

1. In January 1606 Parliament passed a new law. It said that 5 November would become a holiday of public thanksgiving.

2. Guy Fawkes hasn't always been the one on top of bonfires. At different times in history dummies of different people have been burned on 5 November.

3. It wasn't until 1920 that fireworks were added to the 5 November celebrations.

4. For many years the people of Scotton village in Yorkshire refused to celebrate 5 November with fireworks and bonfires.

5. The government decided that the cellars beneath Parliament should be patrolled night and day to prevent another Gunpowder Plot. That patrol stopped a long time ago.

QUICK QUESTIONS

1. At the Civil War battle of Edgehill the famous doctor, William Harvey, settled down with a book as soldiers fell all around him. When he grew cold he pulled what over his legs to keep warm? (Clue: the doctor was no use to them)

2. Charles I was captured by Oliver Cromwell's army and held prisoner in Newcastle. They let him out to play what game in the nearby fields? (Clue: join the club)

3. Charles I went to his execution in 1649 wearing two shirts. Why? (Clue: it was 30 January 1649)

4. Sir Arthur Aston had a wooden leg so he was easily caught in a 1649 Irish battle. He was beaten to death. With what? (Clue: did he put his foot in it?)

5. Oliver Cromwell died in 1658 and the public queued to see his mummified body. But it began to go rotten. What did the government do next? (Clue: you wooden believe it)

6. Charles's head was sewn back on so he'd look good in his coffin. But his tomb was entered many years later and the neck bone stolen. It was used at the dinner table by Henry Halford. For what? (Clue: needed on chops!)

7. In 1653 Nicholas Culpeper wrote that this plant clears bad chests, cures headaches, worms and indigestion, and the juice kills lice in children's hair. What is this wonder plant? (Clue: it cures nothing and has killed millions)

8. In 1660 Charles II returned and punished the men who had had his dad, Charles I, beheaded. One condemned man had his belly opened and his guts lifted out for burning. How did he shock his executioner? (Clue: you can't keep a good man down)

TEST YOUR TEACHER...

How much does your history teacher know about the 1600s? Test them with this quiz — and if they get more than half wrong, threaten them with the Stuart cure for consumption!

1. Why were Oliver Cromwell's followers called 'Roundheads'?
a) because of the shape of their helmets
b) it was an insulting name given to them by the Cavaliers
c) because of their haircuts

2. Which Stuart king was described as 'a nervous drivelling idiot'?
a) James I
b) Charles I
c) James II

3. How did Charles II describe himself?
a) 'the most handsome man in England'
b) 'the King of Elegance'
c) 'an ugly fellow'

4. Who was the leader of the Gunpowder plot?
a) Guy Fawkes
b) Robert Catesby
c) Simon Montfort

5. Prince Rupert, a Cavalier leader during the Civil War, had a dog he took with him everywhere. What breed was it?
a) a black Great Dane
b) an Irish Wolfhound
c) a white Poodle

6. When he was a prince escaping from England (because his father had lost the Civil War), James II dressed as
a) a girl
b) a servant
c) Little Red Riding Hood

7. In the 1600s, who were Stroller's Priests and what did they do?
a) tramps who performed illegal marriages for couples
b) priests who roamed the countryside doing good works
c) thieves who stole from churches

8. What was a 'bung-napper' in Stuart times?
a) a sleep-walker

b) a purse-snatcher

c) a dustman

9. Which of the following was a real 1600s cure for spots?

a) drinking vinegar mixed with chopped-up worms

b) washing in your own pee

c) rubbing in the blood of a freshly killed pigeon

10. Who did Londoners blame for starting the Great Fire of London in 1666?

a) French spies

b) Catholics

c) plague victims

Answers

Superstar Shakespeare

1.a) 2.a) 3.b) 4.b) 5.b) 6.b) 7.a) 8.a) 9.a) 10.a) 11.b)

Anyone who answered c) has a brain like Shakespeare's! (Dead for 400 years.)

Remember, remember...

1. True. People lit bonfires to celebrate and threw dummies on the fire dressed as Guy Fawkes.

2. True. The first record of this was at Cliffe Hill in

London 1606 where a dummy of the Pope joined Guy Fawkes in the flames.

3. False. Within a few years of the plot people began to use fireworks on November 5.

4. True. This village was where Guy Fawkes used to live and the people didn't think it was fair that Guy should take all the blame.

5. False. A search of the cellars is still carried out before the opening of every Parliament.

Quick Questions

1. Corpses. He was used to cutting them up for experiments so he wasn't too bothered about using them as blankets.

2. Golf. A popular game with his family, and granny Mary Queen of Scots enjoyed it too.

3. Charles didn't want to shiver in the cold in case people thought he was shaking with fear.

4. With his own wooden leg.

5. They replaced the corpse with a painted wooden dummy with glass eyes.

6. As a salt cellar.

7. Tobacco. Culpepper even said tobacco ash was good for cleaning the teeth! Ugh!

8. He sat up and hit the man who was cutting him open! That took guts!

Test your teacher

1.c) 2.a) 3.c) 4.b) 5.c) 6.a) 7.a) 8.b) 9.c) 10.a)

INTERESTING INDEX

Where will you find 'bird-droppings', 'chamberpots', 'rhubarb-juice' and 'toad-eaters' in an index? In a Horrible Histories book, of course!

Terry Deary was born at a very early age, so long ago he can't remember. But his mother, who was there at the time, says he was born in Sunderland, north-east England, in 1946 – so it's not true that he writes all *Horrible Histories* from memory. At school he was a horrible child only interested in playing football and giving teachers a hard time. His history lessons were so boring and so badly taught, that he learned to loathe the subject. *Horrible Histories* is his revenge.

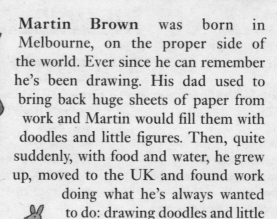

Martin Brown was born in Melbourne, on the proper side of the world. Ever since he can remember he's been drawing. His dad used to bring back huge sheets of paper from work and Martin would fill them with doodles and little figures. Then, quite suddenly, with food and water, he grew up, moved to the UK and found work doing what he's always wanted to do: drawing doodles and little figures.

**HAVE YOU
GOT THE WHOLE
HORRIBLE LOT?**

ISBN 978 1407 10428 7

ISBN 978 0439 94403 8

ISBN 978 1407 10420 1

TROY STORY...

HORRIBLE HISTORIES

GROOVY GREEKS

TERRY DEARY Illustrated by MARTIN BROWN

ISBN 978 0439 94402 1

I GET THE POINT!

HORRIBLE HISTORIES

ROTTEN ROMANS

TERRY DEARY Illustrated by MARTIN BROWN

ISBN 978 0439 94400 7

SEE YOU LATER GLADIATOR!

HORRIBLE HISTORIES

RUTHLESS ROMANS

TERRY DEARY Illustrated by MARTIN BROWN

ISBN 978 1407 10424 9

ISBN 978 1407 10418 8

ISBN 978 1407 10430 0

ISBN 978 1407 10426 3

ISBN 978 0439 94406 9

ISBN 978 0439 94401 4

ISBN 978 1407 10425 6

ISBN 978 1407 10427 0

ISBN 978 0439 94405 2

ISBN 978 1407 10422 5

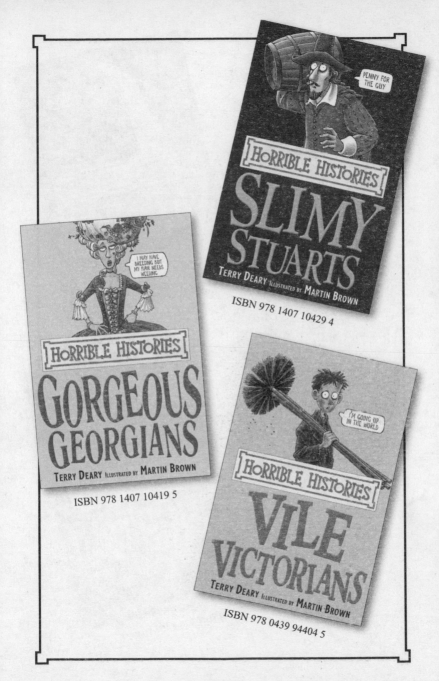

ISBN 978 1407 10429 4

ISBN 978 1407 10419 5

ISBN 978 0439 94404 5

ISBN 978 1407 10431 7

ISBN 978 1407 10421 8

ISBN 978 1407 10302 0

ISBN 978 0439 94399 4

ISBN 978 1407 10343 3

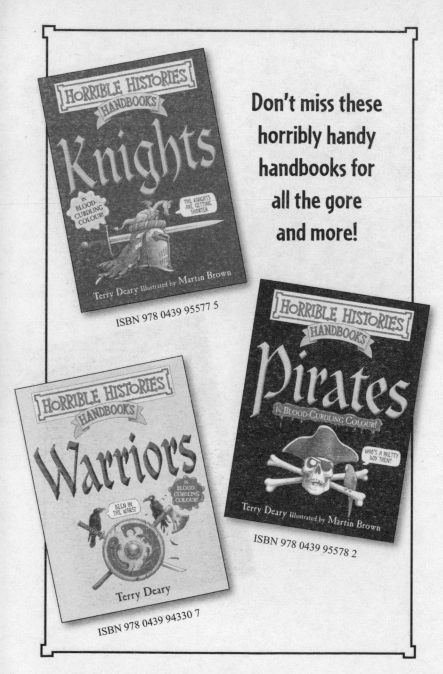

Don't miss these horribly handy handbooks for all the gore and more!

ISBN 978 0439 95577 5

ISBN 978 0439 95578 2

ISBN 978 0439 94330 7

HORRIBLE HISTORIES
HANDBOOKS
Villains
IN BLOOD CURDLING COLOUR!
SEE YOU INSIDE.
Terry Deary Illustrated by Martin Brown

ISBN 978 1407 10305 1

HORRIBLE HISTORIES
HANDBOOKS
Witches
IN BLOOD CURDLING COLOUR!
THERE'S A BAD SPELL AROUND HERE.
Terry Deary

ISBN 978 0439 94986 6

HORRIBLE HISTORIES
HANDBOOKS
THE HORRIBLE HISTORY OF THE WORLD
MUMMY KNOWS BEST!
IN BLOOD CURDLING COLOUR!
Terry Deary Illustrated by Martin Brown

ISBN 978 1407 10350 1

It's top of the pops!

ISBN 978 0439 96382 4

An Awesome Egyptian Pop-up Adventure!